To Catcn
A Horse

Finding the Heart of Your Horsemanship

Amy Skinner

Cayuse Communications

https://cayusecommunications.com

To Catch A Horse:
Finding the Heart of Your Horsemanship
by Amy Skinner

First Printing – September 2019
Paperback ISBN: 978-1-68111-319-7
Cover design by TJ Zark

Printed in the U.S.A.

0   1   2   3   4   5

"As time goes on, all the little things will fall into line. We should be adjusting to fit the horse. Fix it up and let it work. You can't make it happen, and you can't put a time limit on it. You can just set it up to enable him to learn. Sometimes the slower you go, the faster you learn." —Ray Hunt

ACKNOWLEDGMENTS

For pushing me to write a book, holding my hand through the process, and for her tireless efforts in making it a reality, Maddy Butcher; for his insight, information and advice, Stephen Peters; for her generous financial support, Mary Ellen Spaite; for her wise and practical editing, Susan Giffin; for her fantastic design work, TJ Zark; for their guidance and lovely examples, my teachers; for their encouragement and for keeping things real, my family; and for his endless support and humor, my husband Travis.

CONTENTS

FOREWORD

If you know Amy Skinner, you know you are getting a repository of gems in this book. Her knowledge base is broad and has come through numerous sources and been tried and tested with the horse, the ultimate judge of what does and doesn't work.

If this is your first exposure to Amy, you will find one of the freshest and most articulate voices in the horse world.

Over the years, I have watched Amy's knowledge and horse work evolve. She is an insatiable learner. No one wants to follow stagnation and rigidity. Amy is open-minded, and you will be the beneficiary of her hard work and learning.

I give Amy my enthusiastic endorsement because her approach is one that makes horses' welfare a top priority. She is well aware that a learner who is curious, involved, and feels safe is a good student. Amy goes out of her way to make sure these elements are in place for the horses she trains. She understands the neuroscience behind what her horses experience. Based on application, she asks the horse!

Amy is a stickler for making her communication to the horse crystal clear to avoid confusion and unnecessary agitation. She uses her interaction to develop curiosity and involvement, always making sure that the horse is in the right frame of mind to learn.

This is the same approach that she employs with her students, and this is what makes her so special. She engages their curiosity and develops their enthusiasm to learn more, always in a safe environment where they do not feel pressured, hurried or inferior. I think you will find her to be that friendly teacher who is able to present things in just the way that you say to yourself, 'That's exactly what I was thinking or feeling in that situation'. You won't get rehashed phrases here. The reader knows that Amy has been there and done that in her own experience.

You are in for a treat in having her words here to contemplate and put to use for both you and your horse's benefit. If you are like me, I am sure that after reading her book, you will hear some of these comments resonating in the back of your mind, and they will become familiar guides.

I suppose the ultimate compliment is that I know that she understands the horse, and if I needed someone to work with me and my horse, Amy Skinner is on my list.

—Dr. Stephen Peters
Co-author *Evidence-Based Horsemanship*

SECTION ONE:
Philosophy

Integrity: It's What's for Dinner

Integrity

It's not a buzzword; it's a way of life. It means doing the right thing for the sake of doing the right thing, not for credit or to be seen. It's been my good fortune to have had some teachers and parents who were great examples of integrity, and from what I saw with them, and what I've pieced together on my own, here is what integrity means to me:

- Being honorable in what I do and standing behind my actions. If my actions are not right, it means doing what I can to take responsibility.

- It means doing what's right for both the horse and the client, not one more than the other.

- Keeping clients safe is my first priority, and though I won't always give answers that are popular, I will always strive to keep clients safe. It means teaching in a way that my clients can understand, at the level they're at, just like I would teach a horse. We don't judge the horse for its level of education, and we don't make them feel wrong for making mistakes. Teaching people is no different. They have to feel relaxed to learn. It means working a horse the same whether the client is there or not. I wouldn't ride someone else's horse any differently from my own, whether it's worth $500 or $100,000. All horses deserve to feel relaxation and work toward balance. I won't rush anybody's horse because it needs to go to a show, and I won't shortchange a horse because it doesn't have a high-dollar value. It means working for the sake of working, not because somebody told me to get up, but because there are horses that need help.

I don't make my living off of catchphrases, brands, showmanship, or competition, and I try to avoid the rat race altogether. It's hard for me to think kindly of someone who bad-mouths other professionals to get ahead.

The world is what it is, and I can't change that. I went into this business to avoid the chaos of the outside world and find peace, but I realize the only way to contribute is to help. Although I fail my own standards and don't always live up to my ideas of how I should be, I try to remember what Gandhi said, "Be the change that you want to see in the world."

Asking All the Right Questions

We hear "make the right thing easy and the wrong thing difficult," and we feel good about our ideas sometimes. We're giving the horse choices. I've seen this method applied in ways where the horse is forced to choose between two discomforts— the discomfort created outside the trailer, for example, vs. the discomfort of being in the trailer—away from the person and the discomfort it creates.

What if we think about the questions we're asking? What if we're asking the wrong questions, and what if what we want the horse to do is inappropriate or asked incorrectly? What if we make sure the questions we ask have a theme and a goal, such as building trust and a partnership? We would ask very different questions, I believe.

It's not what you say, but how you say it, so the saying goes. If what you ask your horse causes him to lose faith in you, to release him from avoiding you, and to teach him to escape, they are either the wrong questions or you ask them in the wrong way at the wrong time.

We hear that we must be leaders, and that what we say must go. Horses follow, people lead. But being a leader is more than just calling the shots.

Being a leader means intimately knowing who you are leading, and preserving and caring for their needs. It means leading by example, not dictating from the safe seats. It means knowing how to ask questions and to time those questions right to build confidence. Repeated successes build confidence. As leaders, we have the responsibility to set things up so that those we lead can succeed and enjoy doing so.

A good leader does not make anyone—human or animal—do anything, but develops the curiosity and desire for them to do it themselves. A good leader isn't focused on winning or getting credit or looking good, but on instilling the desire to do the right thing.

Does your horse love to follow you? Or does he avoid you and choose the lesser of two discomforts only when you force him to do so? There is a world of difference in what we ask and how.

The Value in a Good Cowboy Story

Years ago, I rode in a colt starting clinic and left ecstatic with the progress my little filly had made. In three days, she had gone from touchy and fearful to calm and fluid. I remember hearing someone complain about how the clinician talked too much, and they wished they had gotten more done.

I thought about the clinic and how my filly had experienced something, been afraid, sorted it out, and sat while the clinician told a story. Then we moved on and repeated this cycle.

For me, and for this horse, there was value in sitting around for a few moments. It wasn't wasted time, but time well spent. I remember watching a road to the horse competition where a clinician said he was going to use the time his horse was resting, after bucking the saddle for quite some time, to desensitize it. He pulled out a leaf blower while that horse stood there, too tired to move and too checked out to even register it. Everything in that deal was rushed, and he had the horse going in a few days but with a swishy tail and pinned ears. How does that benefit anyone?

There is value in silence. There is value in a break. There is value in taking your time with a horse, and there is nothing wrong with taking a step back. Progress is not always linear. You can go up and down and sideways, and you can take a break and listen to a story while your horse sorts out what he thought was going to kill him but didn't.

I have no problem taking a break or going slow or listening to a great cowboy story. It isn't wasting my time or my horse's.

The Trouble with Learning a System

Some of the hardest folks to teach are the ones who have studied a 'system' of training. These methods might work on some horses sometimes, but the ones who don't fit the mold get quickly labeled as crazy, wild, stubborn, untrainable. I used to think I knew what methods to use to train horses until I had a series of horses with which these methods failed. It was hard for me, too, to let go of what I had been taught. The only method I know that works time and time again on every horse is watching the horse's response and adjusting accordingly. That means opening our eyes and ears and listening to the horse.

The horse does not owe us anything. He didn't ask to be here, and he doesn't have to adjust to our way; we have to adjust to fit him so he can get by in our world. After all, we brought him here in the first place.

What Is Feel?

Feel is one of those words that horsemen and women throw around somewhat carelessly. It's ill-defined, confusing, and, to many people, it has this ethereal mysticism surrounding it. I think some people believe feel is unattainable to them, but someday, if they only ride in enough clinics, they can get some of this feel. It sounds to many like they can have this magical experience only if they are super geniuses.

Well, that simply isn't true. And the truth is, everyone is riding with feel. A feel can be anything in between a light touch and a punch. To sound completely obvious, a punch feels like something, right? So, if you're sitting on a horse, you're using feel.

I think a better way to describe the way you're using your aids would be to describe what kind of feel we want in that situation. What you're looking for with horses is a type of feel that just blends, feels good for both partners, and doesn't involve force. If you've ever danced with someone who swept you off your feet, you've experienced this type of feel. If you've had to pound a nail into a wall, and then pet your cat's head, you've used two different types of feel, and you have the capability to adjust to the type of feel each situation required.

Maybe feel can be better described as awareness and togetherness.

Here is a brief description of a situation of feel. I landed in Charlotte, NC, and had twenty-five minutes to catch my next flight to Raleigh. My flight landed late, and the airport was completely packed. Of course, the gate I needed was on the opposite end of the airport, so I speed-walked through the airport as best I could until I got closer to my gate. I could hear the announcement of my flight, and the invitation for different groups to board. People, waiting to board their flights, were spilling out from their gates into the aisleway, and in front of me were swarms of people with no order to the traffic flow going toward me, away from me, stopping directly in front of me, turning around, you name it.

I was desperately trying to get to my gate on time but this unorganized flow of human beings in their own world doing their own things completely blocked my way. I'd see a space open up ahead of me, so I'd speed up, and then the person in front of me would stop suddenly to check their flight information, and I'd slam on the brakes. The person next to me would lose control of their wheel-behind luggage, and it would swing toward me. I'd have to move out of its way and still maintain forward movement. Oncoming walkers, their noses buried in their phones, would almost bump into me, and I'd have to veer out of the way without crashing into the innocent folks beside me. The only thing I had to go off of to get to my gate without running into anyone was feel. It was an interesting experience to say the least, but as I got to my gate, I was quite proud that I hadn't bumped into a single person.

I boarded my plane just before the doors closed and sat in my seat, pondering feel. I think we don't need to frustrate and confuse our horses with erratic requests, but keeping them on their toes creates intense focus. I didn't have time to get frustrated or mad walking toward my gate. I was busy being aware of my surroundings and trying to get from point A to point B without knocking anyone over or missing my flight.

Miracles

I don't mean to be a drag, but sometimes humanity gets me down. I love what I do: helping horses. But after I've fixed up the traumatized horse and sent him back home, I don't always know that he's going to have a better life. I have to watch horses get passed along from situation to situation, and sometimes they end up worse off. I have no control over that. I don't get to decide where they go when I'm done with them, and I can't force the people who own them to stick to what we've worked on while their horses were with me. I can't force people to care enough to take the high road over the easy road, and I watch horses get banged up, dinged up, misunderstood, and frustrated daily.

Of course, I have many great highlights in my job. I get to watch scared horses turn around and trust again. I get to see people learn and turn on their light bulbs. Sometimes I get to watch people change their whole lives.

Those who take the horsemanship journey soon find out it isn't just about riding. It's about who they are as people and what they offer not only their horse but also the world around them. That's the hard part as a teacher. I know I can teach the mechanics, but I can't always make someone want to try when there are shortcuts out there. Not everyone wants to get fit, become aware, get humble, and realize they don't know it all and have so far to go to realize their horse reflects them and their shortcomings. It isn't always a pretty pill to swallow.

Sometimes, I get frustrated with people and wish I could take just horses in training. Horses will always take the better deal if I can convince them it's better than what they're holding. People, on the other hand, are not always so keen to change, even if they see that what I offer is better than what they have. Ego gets in the way. Laziness, greed, lack of interest, you name it. So, when I teach someone who isn't eating it up, dying to get better, willing to go the extra mile for their horse, I feel deflated. I know the horse is getting the worse end of the deal.

A good friend of mine and trainer I really respect told me, "If you love horses, you'll love people." It wasn't so much a statement as a command. Do it. Do it no matter how long it takes. "If you don't commit to changing and helping people, you can never help the horse. It's the people that control that horse's future."

Out of the majority of people I encounter, I can generously say 5 percent want it badly and are dedicated. For most people, it is a hobby, they are interested, yet they are lackadaisical about it, which is understandable. I am only semi-dedicated to rock climbing, for example. I like doing it when it's in front of me, but I'm not dropping everything to go to school and learn everything about it. It's important to find the level of interest they have and get a horse that matches the level of their ability. But I digress.

Sometimes, I meet someone who just wants the easy way out. They bring the horse to me to fix up, like an oil change, so they can go home and keep doing what they're doing. They just plain don't care to learn how to do things better. These are the ones that keep me up at night, make my hair gray. How can I change someone? I can't possibly change someone. I call my friends that I trust, I talk to my parents, I ask the dog for advice. I just sometimes flat out don't know what to do. I have to accept that all I can do is present information and hope for the best. It isn't up to me to change people.

But when I'm just about at the end of my interest in helping these types of people, they surprise me. Not all of them, but a few. Enough. I've had a few doozies turn around and go from hateful and horrible handling to sunshiny and downright emotional the next week. Yes, in one week. It can happen.

I had a student who criticized her horse for an entire hour, told him how stupid he was when he spooked, called him a baby, told me how much better he needed to be. I told her, "He is a reflection of you, and he can go no further." I agonized over saying that. All night, I worried that I had gone too far, but the next week she came back and walked him around on a loose rein, petting him, telling him he didn't have anything to fear. Her horse's eyes were soft, and she was relaxed in her body. I was amazed and asked her what had changed. She looked me right in the eye and said, "I forgot my horse was my friend."

Miracles can happen. They don't always happen, but they can, and they can be so beautiful. I watch horses put out effort and make changes every day, and it always amazes me, but I think the most miraculous is when someone who is set in their ways turns a new leaf. I don't know if I have anything to do with that, but I am honored and humbled to witness it every time.

Live Soft to Ride Soft

Now more than ever before, I've become committed to riding in softness. This means riding in a way that creates suppleness in the horse, willingness, and athleticism, but most of all, developing in the horse an equal interest in our plans.

This means the responsibility is on me to set things up so the horse can succeed, can be supple, and can share my interests. That means the horse can say no, and I have the responsibility to take stock in why, and either ask again in a different way or change the question altogether. It means not 'making' the horse do anything. This is an enormous commitment, and, like any other person, I have moments when I fail at being soft.

It isn't about being perfect all the time, though. It's just about noticing, comparing, and asking why something didn't work and what we can do better, instead of putting the responsibility on the horse to shove him through a movement or action. It's about learning to flow, and in order to be soft with horses, we must live our lives with the same type of flow.

To ride in softness, we have to commit to a life of softness. I tell my students that they can't have one posture in their day-to-day lives, and another posture in their weekly one-hour lesson. What you practice is what you perform, as the saying goes. So, if we are really interested in riding and handling horses with softness, we have to look at our day-to-day handlings. How do we get what we want with our coworkers, boss or employees? Is it through begging, intimidation, pressure, or manipulation? How do we handle ourselves when something doesn't go our way? Do we lash out at others when we are tired, anxious, or upset? Do we communicate clearly with others or assume they think just like us? For sure, all of these reactions will show up in the saddle at one time or another. Softness in life means evaluating every instance and accepting our responsibility in each moment, not blaming others but taking what we can control—our reactions—and honing them.

Living in softness, just like riding in softness, does not mean we live without boundaries. If we clearly communicate our boundaries, and our needs are not met, walking away is not only okay but it may be necessary. Being firm without intent to cause harm to another shows respect for them and ourselves. Similarly, if a horse does not stay within set boundaries made clear to him, it is perfectly okay to close the doors and show him the way again. But this is done without anger or violence, and once the moment is over, we move on.

Just as we take a horse and accept him without judgment, we also should strive to do the same with people. Some horses are flighty, some are quiet, some are sensitive, while others are more tolerant. Through riding in softness, we seek not to make each horse different but to present things to the horse as he is in a way he can accept and understand. Again, the responsibility is on us to communicate to the horse, not to change the nature of the horse. We should try to see people in the same light, full acceptance of who they are, with the understanding we can't change others and their reactions, only ourselves and our reactions.

In this journey, we can't look at situations as if we have failed or succeeded but only in terms of growth. The horse never fails when he doesn't do what we want, he tells us only that we need to change our presentation. In the same way, we don't fail in our lives, but life does tell us we need to adjust how we react or adjust our presentation.

The Horses Who've Been My Friends

A lot of horse trainers are said to have a 'way' with horses. They have methods and tricks that get results, but how many horse trainers do you know whose horses love them? I don't just mean obey them. Does your horse love or even like your trainer? Or you?

Horse training seems to attract people who have a need for control, authority, and recognition. It's easy to impress a crowd by showing all the cool things you can make a horse do, even at Liberty. But not many people are wowed by slow, methodical work that builds trust and a real friendship. I hope my work with their horse makes them feel more confident, more relaxed, and also more powerful, and that I am an asset to him, not something in his way. That is how I build a friendship.

When my new-to-the-horse-world husband and I first started dating, he came with me to a horse show. He was horrified by the warmup ring and even more horrified when it came time for folks to load their horses back up. All the yelling, name calling, and force was something he hadn't seen a lot. "Don't any of these people actually like horses?" he asked me. It's a valid question that I still don't know how to answer.

It's been commonly said, "You have to be the horse's boss before you can be his friend." It's also commonly said, "There is a thin line between respect and fear." It's true that good leadership sometimes means doing the necessary but unpopular thing. A horse that has been spoiled may not love everything you do for a while. But when I sit on a horse, I never lose sight of the fact that I am at the mercy of his strength. If we are not friends or aiming toward becoming friends, what real control do I actually have?

What's in it for the horse? Why should he come around or do anything we say? He doesn't get paid for work like we do, even when we don't love our bosses. And 'because I told you so' does not always hold enough weight with a 1200-pound animal.

It's unfortunate that horses can sometimes be bullied or made to respond through fear tactics because of how nature made them.

Does your horse love to be ridden? Mine doesn't always love it, but it's my goal, and when they don't, I have to think, 'Is he just still struggling with something that he'll come out better for, and do I need to wait longer, or do I need to change something so he can love it?'

I love riding, and if I didn't love riding, it wouldn't be worth doing. Shouldn't my horse love his life with me?

Horses make wonderful friends. They're honest, hardworking, and patient enough to teach us endlessly till we figure it out.

Growing up, I didn't love everything my parents did. I had my own ideas about what I thought I should do, and often I was wrong. But my parents are my friends, even after all the naughty or misguided ideas I had. Sometimes, my mom calls me to tell me she loves me. "But the best part," she adds, "is I actually *like* you."

There couldn't be a better compliment.

The Cons of Being a Good Student

Over the years, I've interned and studied under many great teachers. I've studied hard and tried my best to please my teachers. But teachers aren't always right, and the person giving instruction on the ground, no matter how well-meaning, does not have to bear the consequence of injury. The student does.

I always say to my students, "What I am telling you is just my interpretation of what I see your horse needs." That means I could be wrong, or what I would do in that moment may not be right for them. They have to assess their ability, confidence level, and understanding of the instruction. There are many ways to work at something, and though they may need to push their boundaries, listening to their gut is an important lesson.

The past few years of trial, growth, and a handful of injuries have taught me a lot about rushing, riding green horses before I'm ready, and working on a set schedule. I've had plenty of time laid up from work with my arm bandaged up to think about what this means.

The phase of my life called 'being a good student' is over. 'Being brave' is done, too.

The phase of my life called 'listening to my gut and being smart' has just begun.

Now my interest is learning from my own instinct. I throw out pressures to ride a certain way or to get a horse going at any rate other than his and mine.

For every time I've been told to 'grow a pair,' for every time I've heard "Haven't you ridden him yet?"

For every time I have had something to prove.

For every time I cheapened my horsemanship and ignored what the horse needed just to get a job done or keep a client, I remember it's my career, my well-being, and my conscience on the line. Nobody else's.

Now the only one pushing me is myself and my horse.

I encourage you to do the same. Take all teaching with a grain of salt. Be a horse pleaser and a conscience-pleaser, not a people pleaser. Because after all, it's only money, and it's only time. What do you have without your health, your peace of mind, and your relationship with your horse?

How to Be a Good Student

I have taught around the country and seen all kinds of people with all kinds of goals, riding all kinds of horses. I have students of all ages, income ranges, and disciplines, even some with physical disabilities.

What I've learned is that it doesn't matter what kind of horse someone has, what financial situation the owner is in, what their age or physical limitations are. The folks who make real progress are the ones who want it, show up, do the work, and are teachable.

What does it mean to be teachable? I'm a student, too. So, from one student to another, here are some tips:

- Don't spend valuable lesson time telling your instructor what you know or what you do. It's likely your instructor can see your habits right away and easily determine your skill level. The time you spend sharing these details with your instructor wastes time that she could use for actual instruction.

- Be open to criticism. Don't take any of it personally. Your instructor is doing her best to help you. However, if you find she is overly critical without giving positive direction, find a new instructor. Listen more than you talk. But ask questions freely, and if something doesn't make sense, don't be afraid to ask for clarification. Chatting about unrelated things can take away from the time an instructor has to help you, though a little small talk can help ease nerves or keep students relaxed.

- Do mention health problems, fear issues, and other safety-related concerns to your instructor.

- Be willing to work hard. You don't need to break a sweat over every lesson to make progress, but spending lesson time making excuses for what you can't or won't do makes it hard for the instructor to help you advance. A teacher can only lead you to knowledge. It's up to you to turn that into progress.

- Do take your horse into consideration. You probably know your horse better than anyone else, and if the work seems too much for your horse, say so. A good instructor has a sharp eye for a horse's expression and needs, but they don't know your horse's history of lameness or any ongoing issues. Be your horse's advocate.

Being a good student is probably harder than being a good rider. Learning in front of someone is a very vulnerable step to take. I have tremendous respect for anyone willing to give self-improvement a try, especially in a public setting like a clinic.

A lesson or clinic is a great time to:

- be open-minded
- try new things
- expand your comfort zone.

It is not a time to:

- show off
- worry about how you look
- let your ego get in the way.

A good instructor should make a clinic or lesson a safe place to experiment in and should not make you feel the lesser for making mistakes or for what you don't know. In both riding and horsemanship, I've been a student longer than I've been a teacher. Any success I've had in teaching I owe to also being a student. I still take frequent lessons, and while I'm more selective about who I ride with, I usually find that I do not know enough.

Following Your Dreams Is Not for Sissies

There is this idea that following your dreams is this exciting, sexy journey. In reality, following your dreams means shoveling snow, mud and poop, working terrible side jobs to make ends meet, getting bucked off, crying in your truck, considering some other shady but lucrative profession, but putting your nose to the grindstone each and every day anyway. It might mean criticism from some, admiration from others, but not getting distracted by either. It involves endless learning from your mistakes, from other people's mistakes, and from the horse. It means pure dedication to the craft at all costs.

Following your dreams is not for sissies.

There is no 'end,' no 'arriving.' You are an endless apprentice. Each day, I am grateful to the horses I've known that have molded me—the tough ones, the scared ones, the dull ones, the not-quite-wired-right ones, the incredible athletes, the regular horses, the old ones, and the young ones, all have taught me so much. And I'm thankful every day, horrible and beautiful weather alike, for the opportunity to ride another horse or eight or ten or twelve.

Advice I Cannot Accept

Advice on best trainer practices heard over the years from my colleagues:

- Control your online content
- Censor what you say
- Don't ever, ever come across like you don't know something

I tried this for a while and felt insincere and cheap. As my students ran into their own struggles, I felt I couldn't help them if I couldn't share my own failures. I realized that some trainers and teachers like to portray themselves as all-knowing, while the students, at times, feel hopeless, as if their humanness is preventing them from getting better at riding.

One day, I just dropped the act.

In my articles and social media presence, I have been candid about my struggles, failures, and successes. I started sharing my failures with my students and writing about my own struggles as I developed my career. For me, it's important for my own development, as well as others, to look our egos in the face. Everyone has one, and at best we can 'not disturb the sleeping dog.'

Sometimes, we get humbled. Sometimes, we struggle to accept lessons or we miss them. No one is exempt from the journey, unless we simply refuse to accept our own flaws.

Teacher and student alike are learning, and one is not better than the other.

When we're willing to get down to the nitty-gritty of our inner selves and really look at our habits and beliefs, then we can make real and lasting changes. I'm right there with you.

I realized through watching my own teachers that some were very concerned about their dress, words, and image. They wore appropriate attire, said things that sounded good in public, and maybe rode nicely in front of a crowd. But as they got comfortable with me, and the crowd left, their true colors would show. Impatience for horses' mistakes, insecurity, lack of understanding, or a temper with horses or students.

Some of my teachers showed true compassion to horses and humans at all times, whether we were talented or not, the horse was well bred or well educated or not, or whether the situation would make the teachers look good or not. These teachers walked the walk in all places in their lives. They treated others with respect and did not seem overly concerned with their public image. I realized after some time with these teachers of both kinds that what I wore mattered little, and what I said mattered less if I couldn't back it up with my action and behavior.

My test now in my dealings with horses and students:

- Would I do the same thing now if others weren't watching?

- Would I do the same thing with this horse if there were no 'glory' or public praise for doing it?

- Do I treat the beginner with the same type of respect as the advanced student?

- Do I deal with riders' issues with compassion?

- Do I ever make people feel badly?

- Would I do the same quality of work if the pay was less?

My role models left an enormous and important impression on me. Teaching and training isn't about making money. It isn't about getting the public to be impressed or getting good press. It's about helping horses and helping people. That means teaching and training has plenty of unglamorous moments, hours of basics that may be boring to watch. No dust flying, no tears, no showmanship. Just peaceful quality work between a horse and a human. That is work that makes me proud.

What's Wrong with Covering up the Symptoms?

Usually after a clinic, I feel energized, encouraged, and excited. The energy from a group of people making changes, learning, and discovering gives me a feeling of hope that carries me forward, despite the junk that prevails in the horse industry. Having people help each other, help their horses and themselves is extremely rewarding, and I feel honored to be a part of people's experiences. The fact that these people are here at all tells me that even though a large part of the horse industry disregards the horse in the pursuit of money, fashion, or a quick fix, there is a flickering light of good horsemanship growing.

Sometimes, though, after a clinic I feel drained. There are times when a situation calls for my all. The moment asks me to reach deep inside myself and give everything I have physically and emotionally. It can be very personal, and I may need to give a lot of myself to prove a point or help someone in their particular part of their journey. There have been times when I have cried with people, listening to stories that may seem to have nothing to do with horses at all, but it does. This journey toward working with horses in lightness is really about changing our lives. I've had to pull up things inside myself that weren't pretty or enjoyable to look at as people went through theirs. This is all part of it, pulling up the undesirable pieces of ourselves to become better people. The horses in our lives are limited by what we have to offer inside ourselves, and, to me, being a better person means being a better horsewoman, as well.

From time to time, I meet someone who doesn't understand the value in this type of journey. I don't have any interest in getting followers or fans or having people learn 'my' method, or even really trying to change the way people think. I'm interested in presenting things in a way that makes sense to the horse to the best of my knowledge. What people do from there is their choice. Those who hunger for a better deal with their horse will take it and build on it. If that isn't everyone's cup of tea, I can't change that and wouldn't want to force my opinions on anyone. What I'm offering in a lesson or a clinic doesn't come from me. I can't take credit for it. It comes from the horse and my human interpretation of it, which of course leaves room for human error. But what I'm talking about is my best understanding of the horse and what it needs.

My mare was once ridden in a "B.O.B." (Big Ole' Bit), which she began gaping at the mouth to avoid. She was then put in a flash noseband to keep her mouth shut. After she couldn't avoid the bit by opening her mouth, she began tossing her head up, and then she was equipped with a nice, short martingale to prevent that behavior. What this created was a racing, forehand-heavy, pissed off horse that had the most overdeveloped under neck I've ever seen, and one that was about ready to kill the entire world. She was upset, frustrated, scared, and not interested in listening to anything anyone had to say. She'd been argued with, shut down, and disregarded as an intelligent being with a high sense of self-preservation. Not only is this sad, but take all that gear off, and that was one dangerous animal. (I truly believe she was dangerous in that gear, too).

So, in comes 'horsemanship to the rescue,' and I put a snaffle bit on her. She goes from a ton of pressure to a nice little snaffle bit that makes me feel better. Does she run through that bit? You bet, but she was running through the rest of her old gear too, to a lesser extent. So, the problem is there in both sets of equipment. What needs fixing is not the bit, but her idea of how to operate in relation to the equipment and the humans working it. I had to teach her that I wasn't going to argue with her, but I would wait patiently until she made the correct choices. Yes, it took years. It's better not to start them that way. And she'll probably never feel as nice or light as a horse that was started in a way that they could understand from the beginning. But it was worth it to me, and she's an incredible horse.

Someone recently asked me, after a conversation about bits and why I chose not to depend on a 'stronger' one to prevent unwanted behaviors, "What's wrong with covering up the symptoms?" I had explained that the bigger bit would not solve the root problem, only mask the symptoms, maybe for a while. So, why is this all worth it? What's wrong with covering up the symptoms, as opposed to fixing the root problem?

Well, first the ethical reasons: It treats the horse as a disposable 'thing' instead of a creature with thoughts and feelings and needs. It's like saying, 'If this doesn't work out, I can always put Band Aids on it for a while and eventually just get another one.'

It often puts the horse in pain which can lead to physical problems in the future. My mare has limited range of motion in her back, fetlocks, neck, and fused hocks. She had this starting at a very young age. Physical issues can range from anything as simple as mouth pain to pain throughout its body.

The horse in pain can never develop to its fullest potential in terms of physical ability. It can never work in balance in its body, develop correctly as an athlete (bracing against equipment creates imbalanced musculature), or develop a relationship with the rider. What an unhappy life for the horse that can never develop his talents and feel in harmony with his life with people.

For some people, these reasons may be enough. But the biggest reason is safety.

A horse that is trained through pressure and pain response will never be truly safe. One that is avoiding pain or pressure or responding out of fear can't be reliable. Fear is all-encompassing, as anyone with anxiety or panic attacks is familiar with, that fear is your only focus. The rest of the world becomes drowned out. The only horse that is truly safe is one that is mentally relaxed and taught to connect with the rider or handler, because he feels safe. I have had horses not only relax and move and work better but also save my life (including my mare I mentioned before). If you're working toward creating a partner that isn't in fear, the possibilities go beyond a light, enjoyable ride. You can create a friend and partner, and the things the horse is willing to give back can be truly humbling and incredible.

Limping Along and Working on a Feel

Recently, I sprained my ankle getting on a squirrely horse from a fence. He was straight and right under me, so I threw my left leg over him and rubbed him a bit. He was sort of tight but seemed okay. Then suddenly, he flew backward. I was safely on the fence, of course, and able to roll his hind end away and keep him with me. But in the process, I rolled my right ankle in the fence and sprained it badly.

I've limped along for months, and while it hasn't completely healed, I've been too stubborn and too broke to go to a doctor and have it checked out. But that's beside the point.

My point is sometimes walking around is not my favorite thing, chasing a horse around in the pasture to catch him is not so easy, and walking a mile or two to get my horse handy in his groundwork is not that great, either. I discovered quickly which of my horses operated on a feel and which ones didn't. I discovered where I had been cutting corners and where I had been relying on strength and pressure to get a horse to work with me.

At the end of one day, I learned a lot about horsemanship. I wanted all my horses to work on a float and to help me out, to walk slowly with me, to lead right up to me so I could get on, to find me in the pasture so I didn't have to hobble around, and to hang on and wait while I gimped up into the saddle. What's important when you're feeling well is an urgent priority when you're not 100 percent.

I learned to work with my horses in such a way that they understood and were willing to fill in a little where they could. We can't force cooperation on any horse, and we certainly can't dominate love and respect into any horse. We can put enough heat on a horse to get what we want, but when we're tired, weak, down and out, hurt, or old, the same methods that got us what we wanted are no longer viable. So, start now, while we're young and on two good legs, and work with our horses so we can limp along and lean on them for support.

One of the most amazing men I've ever heard of, Bill Dorrance, rode right up until he died at the age of ninety-three. I admire photos of him in his old age, sitting tall and riding on a float up in the bridle.

Children are amazing, sometimes reaping better results than educated adults with formal riding training. They know what they want, and with their innocent expectation, they produce a pure and honest result. They lack strength, and often they lack timing and technical skill. But they often have just that missing ingredient we as adults often lack, despite our systematic education.

What lacks in many of us is openness and pureness of intention, uncluttered by rational thought. I think the word feel is often mistaken for a type of touch, though it can be, but intention is the most important part.

As Bill Dorrance said in his book, *True Horsemanship Through Feel*:

"Horses are intelligent and they can make decisions. This is the reason that they can sense what a person wants them to do and will try to understand a person's intent. Through his natural instinct of self-preservation, a horse will respond to two kinds of feel that a person can present. He will respond to a person's *indirect feel*, which means that he will either react to or ignore a person's presence—*and how a horse responds depends entirely on the person.*"

The Problem with Training

The problem with horse training is that society is set up to make people believe that they can buy a service and have things the way they want in a certain timeframe. People look at horse training as if they're spending their money on a product. And yet, even the best horse trainers will tell them the horse takes its own time, and no one can guarantee a horse will be doing what they want from him when they want it from him. The other problem is that even if their trainer can get it done with their horse, it doesn't necessarily mean that they can. Getting a horse right takes commitment from them to develop the same type of relationship that the trainer has, otherwise how can they expect their horse to give them what it gives the trainer, when she has put in the hours and sweat, the patience and the desire to get along with their horse? They aren't spending money on a tune up for their car that they can take home and drive.

The fact that money is involved leads people to believe they deserve something for their investment, and they do, but it happens in the animal's time, not the human's. I think any good trainer would say she would do this for free if she could, just to help horses and people. And yet, we all have to eat.

Got Grit?

Everyone knows it takes work to become good at riding. It takes many hours, a good coach, wads of dough shelled out, hours of feeding and caring for the horse, fitness, flexibility, knowledge. Everyone who rides knows how time-consuming the little hobby called horseback riding can be. But it takes more than just time, more than just money. It takes more than natural talent, a good instructor, the right horse, an indoor arena, the perfect saddle, the best feed money can buy, and so on and so forth.

To really get good to where this stuff 'clicks' and becomes part of our own heart and soul, it takes a little thing called grit.

I'm not talking about becoming the type of good where we ride like a trained monkey around an arena with some old German guy in breeches giving us instructions to follow, although having instruction is important, and there's nothing wrong with that. I'm not talking about the type of good that gives us ribbons and trophies to take home, although there's nothing wrong with that, either.

I'm talking about being a real RIDER. A problem solver, a thinker, a feeler, and a doer. The type of rider who can take what she learned in the lesson from the lady in breeches to the open field and try to carry out the same feeling. The type of rider who can understand why her horse is doing the thing it's doing and can work through it. Or at least try to work at it, or better yet, prevent problems in the first place as often as possible.

Grit can't be taught. It can't be given. It can't even be bought with scores of lessons.

It has to come from within us. We either are born with it or work to develop it, or some combination of both.

Grit means we are determined to learn, get better, and do what it takes to get there.

Grit means we tough it out in bad weather, and we don't just quit riding because it's cold.

Grit means we find an education in the bad rides, the tough horses, the poorly built horses, and rough situations.

It means we're willing to get up day after day and keep trying, even if we feel like we're just never going to get better. (But we *will* get better.)

It means we live to learn, and we love the process of learning, which includes fumbles, tears, falls, and frustration.

Grit is not the same thing as stubbornness, refusal to change plans when things aren't working. But it does mean we are developing the strength of character, mind, and body to get to where we want to be, and we will stop at nothing to get there.

Though the approach today is totally different, the image of the buckaroo riding the bucking bronco represents the old attitude of mental toughness, a stick-to-it-iveness that seems to have been lost over the decades.

I think today's society is so focused on comfort, convenience, and fast results, we forget the benefits that a little strength of will can bring.

Whether we're a classically trained dressage rider, a hunter, a cowpoke, a backyard rider, a pleasure rider, it doesn't matter. Our mental strength is what will make the difference between the perpetual amateur and a real rider.

A Journey into the Soul

This past week, I took a course on halter starting in Amarillo, TX, with Brent Graef. It was an incredible time learning to handle young horses that required me to be smooth and clear and to provide support in the right ways at the right time. I learned a lot about providing enough support so as not to abandon the young horses, but not so much that it was micromanaging or overbearing. (My mom says parenting is the same deal, but I think she had a way harder job. Horses can't talk.)

I learned way too much to write all in one blog post. But at one point when I had been working with my eighteen-month-old colt that I named Comanche after the Indians who had once claimed the area as their territory, when I realized what a commitment this stuff really is. A few short days ago, he had never been touched by or been around a person, and now he was looking to me for support and letting me handle him. What that meant was that I had a responsibility to help him keep feeling the lead rope and not lean on it, to be on my game all the time and be smooth, aware, and help him to keep finding the slack. This little guy had never experienced tension in the lead rope, dullness or disrespect, and had no reason not to trust me so far. That also meant that I had a huge responsibility to keep him out of trouble and to keep preparing him for all the new things he would experience in life so as not to break down that precious trust.

I realized while working with Comanche that this horsemanship stuff is so much more than just good reflexes, knowledge of the horse, and smooth rope and rein handling. I had to be centered to help him, and I am still on that journey to be more centered, so I can have something to offer horses. Just having skill isn't enough. As Brent modeled, we have to be quiet inside, to be still enough to listen and observe, and we have to be able to offer real peace to the horse. To do that, we have to have peace with ourselves.

I thought about how many times I had worked with a horse and expected so much of him but had no peace to offer him. How many times, I wondered, had I micromanaged or left horses completely to their own devices in an attempt to be soft? How do I find that balance with each new horse on each new day?

Willingness to experiment is important, but I think having good feelings for the horse and a dedication to do my best for the horse can mean the world and be the difference between making something effective or not effective.

All the horsemen and women I respect and hope to emulate have this 'something' going for them. It isn't just skill. It isn't just whose name they drop, it isn't what kind of horse they ride or how big their hat is or how expensive their rig is. It's definitely not how many ribbons, buckles, and trophies they've won. What really captivates me is someone who walks the talk and strives to be a better person daily to have something to offer not just the horse but the world. Any lasting education I've received has come from these types of folks who have 'it'— folks who catch your attention and make you think, 'I want that, and I'm dying to learn how to get it.'

I think the horse feels the exact same way in the presence of someone who has a heart pure enough to offer.

Learning How to Learn

Learning is not just about absorbing new information and putting it into practice. Those of us who have taught lessons or taken lessons know all about that. In the process of receiving information and digesting it, all sort of foibles can creep up.

Our experiences throughout our lives can set us up to struggle to learn sometimes. Some of us feel stupid, unconfident, embarrassed, resentful at suggestions, small, worried about how we look, afraid to try, scared because of past experiences, or feel like we need to prove what we know and to be right.

We also have to contend with the struggle of learning new information that makes us face our old beliefs. At this point, we have to decide if what we thought we knew measures up to what we are currently seeing, and accept that, though we spent a lot of time learning the mistaken beliefs, we now need to ditch them in order to grow. Habits are hard to break, but accepting what we don't know can be even harder.

Learning to balance ourselves is crucial, and dealing with our emotions in a healthy way and not directing them toward the horse can take a lot of practice to master. Years ago, a teacher told me I needed to "leave my emotions at the door" when I arrived at the barn. I interpreted this as stuffing my emotions down and pretending nothing was wrong when I had a bad day. This obviously made working with my horses incredibly hard; many of them were nervous around me or began ignoring me. It couldn't have felt too good for them to be around that type of feeling. Horses also don't enjoy being around someone whose emotions are out of control.

We have to be willing to accept our mistakes and failures, and this can hurt. It's easier to ignore them, but without acceptance, we can't have growth. We can't be too negative about our abilities, either, because without noticing our improvements, we can't build upon them. There's quite a delicate balance between confidence without blindness to error, and awareness of error without becoming self-deprecating. It's a tight rope, and I often fall on either side. We have to accept that we will never 'arrive,' but that learning is a scary, painful, wonderful, enlightening, and beautiful journey that ends only when we stop breathing.

Learning is so much more than sitting down with a notebook and a pen, watching a DVD, or attending a clinic. We have to do more than just show up. We have to reach inside ourselves and look at every piece, rearrange, or delete what isn't desirable and make room for what we want in there. It's about trying to be a better, more centered person.

Most of us were drawn to horses because they spoke to us. We crave the type of connection horses so generously give us. Throughout our bumpy ride to knowledge, it can be tempting to walk away from self-development. But I think riders who have felt just a taste of this connection know there's more to be had, will be willing to open their hearts and minds to the horse, and to take on the monumental task of learning—and everything that comes with it.

What Is It to Learn?

We all say we want to get good with our horses, and most of us aren't born geniuses. We need some help learning. Whether we find someone we want to emulate—a clinician, an instructor—or just observe the horses we ride, we have so many opportunities to learn. But just because we take lessons doesn't mean we are learning. We have to be teachable first in order to learn. Are you teachable?

First, we have to be willing to admit what we're doing might not be the best way or that there is more after what we're already doing.

We have to be willing to honestly assess our situation.

We have to be willing to listen more than we speak.

We have to be willing to try new and maybe scary things.

We have to be open to trying things we might not have considered.

We have to be willing to drop previous education and see things as they are actually happening, not through a lens we may have worked very hard to develop. This is very common for people who study under a certain someone or follow a 'way.' True horsemanship is about adjusting to every horse.

Can you drop what you think you know and listen? Learning is difficult and humbling. My sincere support goes out to all of you who are trying and stumbling and succeeding and making mistakes day after day. You don't have to be perfect; you just have to try.

When Our Education Gets in the Way of Our Education

Bill Dorrance said, "You can't teach feel, you have to experience it." I like to think I make my living teaching feel, but the reality is feel is sort of elusive. It isn't that some people are born with this magical, mystical ability and others aren't. And it isn't just about education, either. Some of the most talented horsemen and women I know are actually not that educated in the classical sense. I've ridden with some highly educated and beautiful riders who I would not even let lead my horse. I've also ridden with some incredible horse people who flapped their elbows, left their fingers open, and rode with their legs ahead of them like in a chair. But they had the ability to think, feel, and communicate with their horse above all else.

Feel is tricky to teach. I've taken riding lessons since I was six years old, and it's taken me these twenty years to learn that in order to learn, I have to get out of my head. I still don't always do it. Maybe by the time I'm ninety, I'll be where I hope to be, but I've struggled with getting out of my head when taking a lesson. When I'm worrying about what the people on the other side of the fence think, or trying to impress or please my instructor, or feeling doubt about my ability, I am not able to feel. As an instructor, it's incredibly important for me to keep my students in a learning frame of mind, because if they are not in the moment, they are shut off from feel. No one can give them feel, but they can guide you to it.

Feel has a lot to do with observation, open mindedness, and creativity. One of the reasons systems like Parelli and others are so successful is it offers an easy to follow step-by-step approach, removing the guesswork for its students. Even dressage and its levels offers a type of scale which allows people to check their work by. However, if we're openminded and observant, we'll find that these systems and scales don't fit every horse, and if we are going by feel alone, they do a tremendous disservice to many horses, as well as the students going along trying to learn about feel. So, really experimentation and creativity are necessary pinnacles for the avid horseman who has to think outside the box to find the path needed for their horse at each moment.

One of the most difficult things as an instructor is trying to educate people who are already educated. Those with academic careers are often very lineal thinkers, and they can have a hard time thinking creatively. Also, people who read and study riding and horsemanship can get a set idea about what is 'right' in their heads. Riding is so much like art. We can learn all the rules, but a good artist knows when to break them. Feel requires lots of room for mistakes, accidents, and failure. We can't be too concerned about messing up, because we can't know what doesn't work sometimes until we've gone there. We can't know the limits until we've gone too far, and we can never advance until we've pushed.

So, how do we learn feel? No, don't stop taking lessons. Don't stop reading, and don't stop thinking. But get out there and watch the horse. Go behind the barn and try new things; who cares what others think? Don't be afraid to bounce a little, mess up, look stupid, whatever. You think the 'greats' never ruined a horse, got bucked off, cried in their trucks, or went down the wrong road with their horses for too long? Feel requires observation, wiggle room, quiet moments watching, and reflection. Don't be self-deprecating, and don't be pompous. Don't let your education get in the way of your education. Listen to your instructor but throw away what feels wrong. Your horse knows what's best, and if you watch and listen, so do you.

SECTION TWO:
Training

Balance, Trust, and Respect

Balance, trust, and respect are three of the most important elements to me in horsemanship. After attending Brent Graef's Young Horse Handling Class to halter starting yearlings, I've thought a lot about these words. Since the topics are fresh in my mind, I thought I'd elaborate on what they mean to me.

Balance
—Balance on left side of body and right, and left and right eye balance
—Balance from poll to tail: hindquarters, front quarters, and ribcage

—Athletic development and lightness
—Variety in training, developing versatility
—Blending/directing; good riding is a partnership, not a dictatorship. First, we go with him, then he gets with us.
—Balancing, exposing a horse without making it dull, and keeping a horse sensitive without allowing it to be afraid
—Balanced hoof care, dental work, and body work to promote a healthy horse that can work at the peak of his ability
—Developing rider balance and understanding its impact on the horse's balance, constantly striving to be better

Trust
—Figure out what his thoughts are and blend with them.
—Gain awareness of his needs.
—Redirect, not discipline
—Build a connection.
—Let him be right, set him up for success.
—Create an atmosphere for learning.
—Help eliminate fear through thoughtful preparation, not dulling and desensitizing.
—Don't teach him to fight.

Respect
—Respect is not gained through intimidation or mistreatment.
—Respect is earned from the horse, it is not a given.
—Respect is mutual.
—Respect comes from understanding the horse and advocating for it.
—Being a real leader means putting him first and leading through example, not making demands.

 To me, just about everything in my day-to-day work expands on these three elements. If any of them are missing, the work is incomplete.

Bombproof or Shut Down?

Bombproof: the word seems to be a favorite among horse owners. People love to brag about their bombproof horse. Top-name clinicians make gobs of money every year selling desensitization methods and tools. Horse people spend their time desensitizing to anything and everything: plastic bags, flags, tarps, ropes, you name it.

Desensitization is a powerful tool, and if we are going to ride safely or get a job done, it serves a very important purpose. But there is a fine line between desensitization and an absolute deadening of the horse. I believe the reason this line is so often crossed is simple: rider fear.

I'll break this down a bit more. A huge demographic of riders in this country are inexperienced and ride at a beginner to novice level, with little understanding of the inner workings of a horse's mind. That doesn't make them bad. We all have to start somewhere, and I believe that a blank page is a beautiful thing!

What does make that dangerous, however, is when the human's inexperience leads to fear, and fear usually leads to a need for control at any cost. They may fear that if the horse spooks on a ride, they may not be able to ride it out or will be unsure of what to do.

Many people spend endless time and money searching for the 'dead broke' horse that will never spook, buck, rear, etc. It is the horse that rides like a machine and just plods away happily.

Sadly, this horse does exist, but usually at the cost of the horse's mental well-being. Think of the sour, old rent-a-horse many of us have ridden down the trail, or the dull school horse that follows the horse in front of him, regardless of what noise the rider may be making up there.

These horses have been 'desensitized' to death and have learned to ignore everything. They have shut down inside. They are the antithesis of what good riding is about: lightness, partnership, and trust.

Trust is much more important than desensitizing. It isn't possible to expose a horse to every scary thing out there. And who would want to?

What I look for more than anything is for my horse to work with me, and, over time, while developing this lightness and partnership, he begins to trust that I can get him through anything.

It doesn't mean he is no longer afraid of tarps, bags, etc., but it means that when he is with me, he will start to look to me to help him out and feel safe. That also means I have a tremendous responsibility to keep him safe and not put him in a position where he could get hurt or expose him to too much before he's ready.

I'll share a story that I think proves my point: a horse rescue had asked me to help them load an older mare into the trailer to send her off to her new forever home. This old mare fit the description of 'bombproof.' She wasn't afraid of anything. She was also about as braced as they come, stiff, upset, and one of the hardest horses I have ever had to put in a trailer. It was as if this horse had had the life completely dulled out of her over time, and to protect herself, she had shut down.

No amount of flagging, spurring, whipping, etc., will bring life into a shutdown horse, at least not much or not for long. There were moments when she seemed to open up and look like a new horse, starting to soften and become alert. She would lick, chew, and blow, and seem happy. Then she would shut down again and get rigid as a board.

Needless to say, the times when she attempted to load onto the trailer were when she was softening. When she became braced again, as if tying her mind and body into knots, would have nothing to do with me or the trailer. She worked in and out of this softness for a few hours, and while she did load in the end and trailered safely, the knowledge that she carried a lifetime of 'bombproofing' with her still weighs heavy on my mind. Undoing this dullness could take months or years. It wouldn't happen all in a few hours.

I think this old mare is a good example of the result of 'bombproofing.' Nobody knows her exact history, but we don't really need it, because the horse tells us where she is. The bombproofed horse learns to shut out outside stimulus, and the human exchanges life and a willing mind for the illusion of safety—a dull, mindless drone of an animal.

It is the utmost insult to the horse. If we are to pay respect to his nature, we owe it to him to develop better riding skills so we can stay with him when he is afraid or upset, and better feel and timing to bring his mind back to us.

The True Cost of a Thirty-Day Start

This scenario is one that is extremely familiar to me: a client calls and asks me to start a horse. They say they can afford only thirty days, and when I make no promises about a thirty-day gentling, they go somewhere else to get more "bang for their buck."

Then they take their horse to a trainer who will start him in thirty days. The client is amazed with how fast their horse makes progress. The trainer is riding their horse through water, moving cows, standing on their back, cracking a bull whip, etc., etc.

Soon the horse goes home, and the client discovers they cannot catch or ride it without encountering problems.

That's when I get the call: "Will you come fix my horse?"

Often in a thirty-day start, the instructor rushes the horse, and he appears to make significant progress but doesn't gain true confidence. He doesn't have enough time to absorb the information. The instructor doesn't have enough time to build real experience that will translate helpfully to the horse's owner.

It's like the horse had finished a quick kindergarten course, and now must go home to hold down a job. It's the difference between studying for the multiple-choice test versus studying to understand a concept. Return this horse to a non-professional, and the horse is totally lost, like a student with no multiple-choice options.

It takes significantly longer to restore confidence and teach over poor information than it does to build confidence in the first place.

Aside from the mental harm and subsequent repair, consider the math: say thirty days of training costs $1000. Often I spend three to six months rehabilitating a damaged horse. That's $3000 – $6000, often more than what a client may have paid for the animal. That does not include the cost of any veterinary work or body work needed from any physical damage incurred through this rushed training process.

I work holistically, assessing the horse mentally and physically, since tightness and pain contribute to behavioral problems.

When many owners hear this news, they feel dismayed. They now have a horse they can't handle or ride, and they can't afford the fix. This is the reason I own four 'Lost Cause' horses. Their former owners didn't know where else to turn for them, so I took them on. It isn't easy to find a home for horses like these, as not everyone has the time, skill, or financial freedom to spend on horses who need this much help.

Imagine you can't find a home for such a horse. Your options are now to feed and care for a horse you cannot ride, or resort to euthanasia. In the end, either your pocketbook or your horse suffers.

So, how can you avoid this?

First, it's important to take realistic stock of your abilities and financial situation. If you ride only on weekends, is it fair to own a young horse? It may have done well for the trainer because she was riding him consistently, and not well for you because you cannot.

Are you a confident and knowledgeable rider? There is no shame in riding a 'been there, done that' horse. Look logically and honestly at the challenges and demands of having a young or nervous horse.

If you are able or determined to have this relationship work, find a trainer who can honestly assess your ability and your horse's needs. Don't believe any guarantees based on time, as a horse does not work on a person's schedule. Cramming important concepts into this short time can be detrimental to the horse.

Find someone willing to work with you and your horse. Take lessons, come and watch, and when the horse goes home, keep up consistently, and follow through with a good instructor.

The choice is up to you. Time is money, as humans say. The horses say it's the foundation of good experiences and challenges that matter, no matter the time.

Bad Routines

I once worked at a boarding and lesson barn with sixty head of horses. Every day I'd drive up in my little blue Hyundai, 9:00 a.m. sharp. The horses milled in the stalls, their wistful nickers escalating into anxious whinnies accompanied by pawing and kicking out. As I prepared the grain and hauled it down the aisleway, the noise of sixty hungry horses fighting each other through the stall walls was deafening, and I'd hustle to drop grain in buckets. After I had fed them all, there was peace and quiet, for a short time at least, until they'd finished, and they started pawing and kicking back up as they prepared to be let out for the day.

At the time, I didn't know much about horses other than what I'd seen. I didn't know the difference between neurotic behavior and a mentally balanced horse, mostly because I'd come across more neurotic horses than the other type. I grew up riding jumpers that were kept in stalls and had been around lesson horses ridden on the rail in the same order for every lesson five days a week, so stable vices were just a part of being around horses. Some kicked when I rode too near, some had to be brought in if their buddy came in so they didn't run like a tornado turned loose in the flatlands, and some bit when I cinched up. These were just irritating side effects of being around horses to me at the time.

It wasn't until I got around horsemanship some years ago that I saw what horses could do. Until then, I was used to calling out 'door' before entering any arena, trying not to spook any horse being ridden, and tiptoeing around. But suddenly, I was exposed to horses that were ponying other horses, walking calmly through a herd of cattle near a branding fire, going in and out of trailers like it was nothing, and that could gallop, then stand calmly and fall asleep. These were horses that had soft expressions in stressful environments, doing their jobs without fear. They were not the types of horses I'd grown up riding, and I was excited by the possibilities.

Horses are extremely adaptable. They are designed that way by nature; without being adaptable, they wouldn't have survived. There was a time when horses were ridden into war, lowered down into coal mines, transported by boats, and ridden down busy cobbled streets. Nowadays in many boarding barns, you find horses being ridden with ear plugs and drugged to get onto trailers, while wearing shipping boots and helmets. Horses fall apart at any type of change, but this is not how it needs to be. Horses provide us with many opportunities to create well rounded, sane, and productive partners.

In developing my career, I've experimented some with my own horses and the training horses that come through my barn. Leasing a barn gave me the freedom to feed and care for the horses however I saw fit. I remembered the sixty horses threatening to tear the barn down if I fed any later than 9:01, and I decided I'd never have that again. I had the luxury of feeding whenever I wanted, and my horses always got fed any time between 4:00 a.m. and 11:00 a.m., depending on the day and what else I was doing. I rode them in whatever order I could fit them in, and they usually had some job to do, so I could squeeze in tuning up a thirty-day-er at the same time as fixing the fence or getting some fresh colt a little exercise while I rode one of my own poor neglected horses.

My horses became fairly easy to get along with, and any training horse I had went right into the mix. For the most part, everybody found their place in their society, and everybody got along in the same pasture. The results were horses that I could bring alone into the barn to trim without whinnying and dancing around for their friends, and horses that I could easily keep all together, largely without incident. I could take them new places without them losing their minds, and they weren't busting down the stall walls to get fed if I wasn't on their schedule. My life didn't revolve around them and their care, although I do care deeply for them and their needs. But they fit into my life and schedule, and they could help me out in my life instead of needing 'full service' round the clock like many horses do, especially on the East Coast. The results seemed to be a more balanced and easily adaptable animal.

Our society revolves around routines. Most of us work day jobs and have to be there at a certain time, have lunch at the same time, and come home for dinner. We like to watch certain shows, go out for dinner on fish fry night, and on the weekend, we take to the barn. But taking our routine-oriented lives to the horse world can have its consequences. It can create horses that are dependent on these routines and rob them of their natural ability to adapt.

If you walk into your average boarding barn, you'll find horses that have to be taken out in a certain order, fed in a certain order and turned out in certain pairs. Daily life revolves around these routines in which they've been trapped. Trying to break these routines can result in mass chaos. Just try to have that herd-bound horse that always goes out with his buddy in the morning stand for his morning farrier appointment, and you'll see this can be a daunting task.

I urge my fellow horse men and women to try and seek this adjustable, well rounded horse and drop their routines. Don't rush up to the barn to feed the minute your horse whinnies, but have that cup of coffee and feed when you can. Don't get suckered into the same routine bringing your horse in to ride in the same way, bribing him to be still and quiet with treats as you tack up for your ride. Ditch that same mind-numbing warm up and go ride in the hills, or zig zag around the weeds, try to make shapes in the snow. Turn on your own creativity for exercises and engage your own mind to engage your horse's. Tack up somewhere else today. Turn your horses out in a different order. Change things up and explore possible adjustments for your horse. Because there will be times your routine has to fail—maybe a power outage, an emergency, a show, a clinic, or the arrival of a new horse. Set your horse up to succeed for these moments, and you'll find yourself with a more enjoyable, sane partner.

Is Your Horse Ready for Uncertainty?

Prior to Hurricane Florence's arrival, a mandatory evacuation was issued for many communities on the North Carolina coast. The news predicted a catastrophic storm with high winds and flooding.

For several days, I offered transportation to those seeking to move their horses further inland and out of harm's way. On the drive from evacuation areas, I came back with only one horse in my trailer. My offer of help was rejected or thwarted because, in one way or another, owners had not trained their horses for life's uncertainties. But here's the thing: *Uncertainties are Certain.*

Many folks had not moved their horses off their properties in years. Some horses were used to a very set routine and became extremely nervous with hurricane accommodations (for many, a pen or stall was all that was available).

One mare colicked when moved. Another horse's owner rejected my offer for a ride, saying her horse would not load in my stock trailer because he was used to only a slant load trailer. Another would not move her horse because all that was available was a pasture with cows. Still another said her horse could not ride in a trailer with other horses.

Unfortunately, with time pressing before the storm, I left these folks behind. The storm was not good to the coast. A week after the storm, many of those roads were still flooded or inaccessible, making evacuation impossible. I worried many horses are now standing in floodwaters, at risk of drowning, disease, and death.

Lack of preparation and inability to create an adjustable horse undoubtedly resulted in tragic consequences. My heart ached for the animals left behind to suffer and die.

The storm offered a sad, yet important, lesson in preparedness: we don't do our horses any favors by keeping their worlds small. If your horse can't adjust to new sights, routines, and scenarios, the likelihood of him surviving and simply staying healthy through an event like Florence lowers dramatically.

In times of emergency, we cannot afford to be picky. We cannot afford to delay. We need to be able to catch, load, and transport horses quickly. At the very least, they need to be able to tolerate different sights, sounds, experiences, and accommodations.

I make sure to load and transport my horses frequently, even for short trips. During the hurricane, a large tree fell and took down a section of my fence. In minutes, my horses were haltered, loaded, and moved to the neighbors. To them, it was nothing new. My neighbor joked they were just having a 'slumber party,' as we unloaded four horses in the pouring rain.

Wild horses roam miles a day, but domestic horses are often confined to small areas. Some go from stall, to pen, to arena their entire lives. Their world becomes very small, and it doesn't take much to upset their systems.

It pays to build confidence with adjustability:

- Taking him to new environments
- Learning new things
- Riding on different footing
- Feeding at different times

These steps not only help us be with our horse and ride more safely, they could save their lives in an emergency.

If you are working hard now to keep your horses routine 'just so' to prevent stress and colic, stop and ask yourself: What will they feel like when you can't control that routine?

If you just haven't gotten around to taking the time to expose them, are you okay with leaving your horses behind, because they haven't been in a trailer in a decade and you cannot load them?

Do your horses a favor, help them be mentally and physically adjustable enough to tackle whatever comes their way. Mentally-adjustable horses are equipped to survive.

Anatomy of a Brace

Most of us have ridden or handled a braced horse at some point in our riding life. Stiff and resistant horses are, in fact, more common than soft and compliant ones.

Unfortunately, training often focuses on correction rather than offering a feel for a horse to follow. Corrections contribute to brace; they place emphasis on what a horse should not do, rather than on making clear what he should do.

For example, in groundwork, when a horse leans on the lead rope, many trainers will bump or tug the rope to request the horse 'get off' the rope. When trainers feel pressure from the horse, they respond with pressure. It might be effective, but it can often produce concern from the horse or more tension. Sometimes, they end up getting a horse that bobbles in and out of heaviness and over-softness. It's not learning to follow a feel consistently. Instead, it hides from the rider's or handler's hand.

Sometimes, we mistake confusion for resistance. Making a correction when the horse is momentarily confused can be detrimental to a horse's confidence.

I recently took a week-long halter-starting class with Brent Graef in Canyon, Texas. It was a return trip to the Graefs', and this time, I came away with an entirely different concept of softness.

Brent gave us a demonstration of following a feel on a halter and used me as the horse. In a living room, I took the halter in my hands and closed my eyes while he took the lead rope in his hands. Admittedly, I was a little nervous, even though I knew there wasn't any reason for concern. My class was watching me, and I suddenly realized I didn't know the layout of the furniture. I worried I might bump into something or be a 'bad' horse.

He told me to do only what I felt. He did not use words to communicate with me. When I felt a light feel in the lead rope to come forward, I did so but very tentatively. I felt no pull, even though I was walking very slowly, taking cautious steps forward. Another message came through the rope, but I wasn't sure what it meant. I stopped to consider it for a moment. Again I felt no pull, only the steady feel of that very quiet message. I realized he wanted me to turn, so I followed that.

Soon enough, I was relaxing after realizing I was not going to get in trouble for making a mistake. I could have time to process information and experiment. I was following the feel of the rope all over the living room, turning left, right, stopping, and following the smoothest request in the lead rope to take steps back.

I thought I was doing a great job at backing up on a feel, when suddenly I felt a pull forward in the rope. I immediately braced up and stopped. The feel was so disconcerting after the confidence I'd gained that I had the distinct urge to sit down, quit, or run away. I laughed at this thought when I realized it. I was completely trusting him to get around and then felt betrayed by this horrible feeling. It made no sense. It didn't match the other messages he'd given me. I was actually angry for a moment. The pull continued until I stepped forward, but I was so concerned, I opened my eyes and said, "What gives?"

Brent laughed and said, "I was asking you to come forward while you were backing up, and you didn't respond soon enough. So, I pulled you forward."

I was shocked. He went on to explain how a horse can become extremely discouraged by lack of smoothness, by mistakes, or by our lack of patience. His point was suddenly crystal clear. I had been feeling confident, and then I didn't trust his feel. "Let's try again," he said.

I closed my eyes again and reluctantly walked forward with the feel. It took a while to regain confidence, and it never got back to its prior level.

"Now do you understand?" he said.

I did.

He was trying to show us how:

- making a request at the wrong time
- not giving the horse enough time to process
- or making a correction for the wrong reasons in the wrong way

These tiny but significant moves could cause so much damage, especially to a sensitive horse like myself. If I were a horse, I would have taken off in an instant and become very good at it. (In horse-speak, my sense of self-preservation is very high.)

I was suddenly overwhelmed with guilt from a thousand horses who had tried to take off, become heavy on the lead rope after tuning me out, pedaled backward, shot their heads up—all ways they had tried to tell me that my feel was offensive. I thought they were resistant. The thought occurred to me that they were resisting my feel. As usual, the problem was me and my presentation.

The more I learn, the more I realize the problem is rarely the horse.

Fitness

Fitness and core strength are kind of buzzwords that everyone knows are important but kind of brush off, like flossing our teeth or eating our vegetables. We all know it will make us feel better, but it's hard to commit to put out the effort to get there. Getting in shape can be tough, especially for those with a sedentary lifestyle or job that consumes forty-plus hours a week and extra responsibilities. My aim with this book is not to lecture anyone on what they should be doing but just to relate my experience with fitness and eating and how it's related to my riding.

I think horse people are well known for having bad eating habits and long work hours, and I've been no exception. For years, I've skipped breakfast and started my day of riding eight or more horses, cleaning stalls, slinging hay, fixing fences, and teaching lessons on a stomach full of nothing but black coffee. Around lunchtime, I'd be starving, but with plenty of horses left to ride and no desire to feel a bunch of food bouncing around in my stomach, I'd eat something small, like a granola bar or half a sandwich. When my day would end around 7:00 or 8:00 or sometimes later, I'd be famished and sit down to a huge dinner and go to bed. I was always tired, and no matter how many hundreds of bales of hay I threw or mounds of manure I shoveled, I never got any stronger. My back hurt from riding colts and their acrobatics, and at night, I'd have to stretch my back out.

One day, I realized my job was athletic (duh!) and that made me an athlete. Athletes eat and train for their jobs; otherwise, their bodies wouldn't be able to perform. I couldn't believe it took me this long to catch on to this fact, but suddenly, I decided I was going to treat myself like an athlete. I started waking up earlier and making breakfast, eating a midmorning snack, a good lunch, and a lighter dinner. I cut out sugar, upped my protein, and lowered my carbs, with lots of fruits and vegetables. During lunch breaks, I started working out. I did a lot of yoga, strength training, and cardio. The first two weeks were hard. I was always sore, and I was really tempted to quit working out, because it seemed to make riding more difficult with my legs feeling like two heavy tree trunks. But within a month, I felt fantastic. I started to feel stronger and more energetic. After my second month, I noticed huge changes in my riding.

For starters, I have tons of energy. My work doesn't exhaust me anymore, and I don't feel stiff at the end of the day. While I am eating myself right out of my budget, my metabolism is much higher, and I actually feel like the food I eat is giving me what I need for the day, not just filling my stomach and making me tired. As for my riding, I have much better awareness of my body, and so, little problems I had had started to go away— unevenness in my body, collapsing rib cage or shoulder, and slouching shoulders. My posture is naturally much better because my core is stronger. I can go with a horse much better when it spooks, spins around, or bucks, because I have much better core stability, therefore I rely less on my hands or reins for balance.

This healthier lifestyle also has made me a more confident rider because I feel less intimidated by sudden movements and goofy antics from my young or troubled training horses. I am much less reactive and more able to ride out a buck or squirt or bolt and take my time to deliberate what action should be taken. My back does not hurt at the end of the day, and a jarring movement doesn't make me wish I didn't have six more horses to ride.

Another side effect of my fitness progression is that I have a better understanding of bringing a horse along in its own fitness. In my own body, my stiffnesses and weaknesses have benefitted only from more attention. I worked harder on the areas that were weak instead of working predominately on what was easy and already strong. I also made stretching, lengthening, and symmetry a huge priority so that my strength was functional and benefitted my lifestyle instead of just looking better. Exercising in a program that was conducive to these things helped me understand better the amount of time it takes to build muscle, how important it is to strengthen weak areas and become symmetrical to do my job better, and how important these things are equally for the horse.

When training a horse, we can't expect changes to happen immediately, but they should happen slowly over time if we are to build healthy muscle and lasting changes. I also got a sense for when to push a little when a horse was resistant, as I would become fatigued in my own workouts but knew progress could be made if I reached a little deeper. And I found when to back off and give the horse a rest made a little more sense too, because if I worked out too hard, I became stiff and lacked any 'juice' for my next workout, so it became counterproductive.

Sticking with my fitness program at first was tough, but it has been so worth it. Changing my eating habits was probably the hardest because it's so easy to get caught up in tasks and brush off eating, or eat whatever is handy. But once I got in the habit of eating better and more often, my tastes changed, and I stopped craving what wasn't good for me. Yes, my grocery bill has gone through the roof, but I have all the energy I need to do my job. Getting stronger and being more fit has made all the difference. Fitness and healthy eating as a lifestyle is something I wish I'd adopted earlier in my life, and something I will most definitely continue through my riding career. Riding is an athletic endeavor, and I can't imagine doing it without a level of fitness.

One of the Many, Many Benefits of Fitness in Riding

As part of my fitness routine, I try to run two to three times a week. Early on, I was getting winded easily, which I chalked up to lack of cardiovascular fitness and thought it would improve with more running. I also struggled to maintain a decent tempo and sometimes had a sore lower back after running.

My husband and I like to exercise together when we can. He helps motivate and educate me, always showing me how to maintain good form and alignment and ways to use my body more efficiently. I never can keep up with him on a run, and he's always been good natured about slowing down while I huff and puff behind him with legs that feel like lead. Today, he asked if I'd like some help on my running form, and, of course, I was interested.

He showed me how to run on the balls of my feet instead of my heel so that my joints didn't take so much concussion. I learned how to lift my knees instead of dragging my legs behind me. Suddenly, I had better posture and kept myself straighter. The first thing I noticed was that breathing became infinitely easier. I wasn't winded. He explained that the jarring motion of landing on my heels caused my upper body to get compressed under its own weight from the immediate impact, causing my lungs to get compressed for a moment and forcing air out of them. Running on my toes allowed for better shock absorption through my joints and upper body, making it easier to breathe. Because of this, I had more energy and could run farther and faster with less energy exertion.

Another thing I noticed was that my calves, thighs, and butt became tired much faster. This was because I was using my leg muscles to propel myself forward, rather than dragging my legs onward. I didn't feel any pain in my lower back or knees, just muscle fatigue from muscles that weren't used to as much work. Though my muscles were growing tired, I still felt like my whole body was being used much more efficiently, and running became much more of a pleasurable experience. I felt like I had a brand new take on it, and instead of dreading it, I suddenly looked forward to running.

The whole time, I kept thinking with amazement about the horses I train that feel heavy in the bridle, get winded easily, or seem lazy. So many of these horses are in the habit of using their bodies inefficiently, and in order to perform the tasks we ask them, they have to use so much more energy. They become dull, resentful, or just tired. Once they start to learn better ways of carrying themselves, their whole attitude often changes. Things feel better, and they start to look forward to their work instead of resenting it. And they start developing the muscles they need to carry themselves correctly, a little at a time. As long as we allow them frequent breaks to help with muscle fatigue, their experience can change quickly from unpleasant to very enjoyable for both horse and rider.

I encourage all my students to find themselves a fitness routine. It helps plenty with riding, and if they want their horse to use his body correctly, it's absolutely imperative that they aren't in his way. Their own physical imbalances and weaknesses block the horse from developing symmetrically as well as reinforcing their imbalances.

Aside from this, embarking on a journey toward fitness allows a rider a better understanding of what a horse goes through physically while trying to do what we ask. To be fair to our horses and to get better, lighter results, we need to understand why they're struggling and how to help them carry themselves better. As we experience our own body's strengthening and balancing, we can learn so much about how to better connect to them physically.

Bad Words

I have a bone to pick with you, horse world.

There are a few words that I really, really dislike hearing. I hear them a lot. I think of them as very bad, dirty words which one should never say in front of their mother or riding instructor.

Here are two of them:

- Stubborn
- Lazy.

People say all kinds of things about their horses, some anthropomorphizing their behavior and personalities. ("He's so outgoing and friendly!" "He loves meeting new horses!" "She's selfish and grumpy!") Others make excuses for their lack of communication by blaming their horses. They decide it's the horse's trait that's in the way, and it sticks easily since the horse obviously can't explain himself (at least in English). So, people call their horses stubborn, lazy, stupid, grumpy, etc. I don't spend much time around people who call their horses stupid, and I plan to keep it that way, but I do hear stubborn and lazy quite often.

And so, I would like to say, as a really great teacher of mine Alicia Byberg says often, "Pet your horse and slap yourself." (I remember that saying often and think it's genius, and it also sucks to hear!)

Everything your horse does happens for a reason. It may not make sense to you at the time, but to him, it makes perfect sense. Otherwise, he wouldn't do it.

So, if he isn't loading, isn't going forward, isn't moving, isn't whatever you want him to do, ask yourself why, and think from his perspective.

- Listen
- Feel

And get some help from someone who understands horses.

But if progress with this equine is what you want, drop those words like a hotcake, and fast. They don't help, and all they do is get in your way of seeing the whole picture.

As many great horsemen have said, "The horse is never wrong." He is either doing what he thinks he is supposed to do or he's doing what he thinks he needs to do to survive. (You have trained him to do that through repetition, on purpose or on accident. It doesn't matter whether you realize you're doing it or not; he is learning.) So, you have either blocked him or taught him to disrespect you. He has no idea what to do, thinks the trailer is going to eat him, and your lack of patience, coupled with the terrifying dark space of the trailer, makes him need to get away no matter what.

Maybe he doesn't go forward because your body is tight, and it blocks him from feeling free to move, or you are sitting too far forward, or your reins are too tight, or he is frustrated with what you're asking him to do, or something hurts, or his body is tight from teaching too many lessons, or he's been in a stall too long. There could be billions of reasons. But lazy is not the horse's way. I hate hearing when people say, "Horses are inherently lazy." They are not. They seek peace, not freedom from having to do anything. I think that's a huge misconception and an unkind way of looking at the animal that we spend hours riding around on or making our livings off of or enjoying however we do.

So, if you find yourself saying something about your horse that doesn't sound nice, stop and think about it. Why would he act that way? Could there possibly be a reason that we hadn't considered yet?

I think it's surprising the amount a horse is willing to give when we make the changes he needs so he can get along with us. He'll give a lot, even if we still don't have everything together. I know I certainly don't have everything together, and some days I feel bad for the way I rode.

But at the end of the day, it's important to look back and reflect: Why did my ride go well/poorly/so-so? What could I have done to change that?

And let's remember what smart horse people often say, "When somebody talks about a horse being stupid, it's a sure sign that animal has outfoxed them."

Please Don't Pet My Horse: A Word About Touch

People who come to my barn are probably befuddled by my posted sign: PLEASE DO NOT FEED OR TOUCH THE HORSES. While many of my clients are familiar with my request that my horses not be hand fed, for reasons I will get to here, no petting to some might seem a bit harsh or confusing. I'll try to illuminate this seemingly odd request.

Some people are extroverted. Some are introverted. Some people like to hug, while to others the thought of being touched by a stranger makes their skin crawl. Anyone requiring a larger 'bubble' knows the discomfort of being forcibly snuggled by a well-meaning person without feel for their body language. People omit feels just the way horses do, which are either inviting, closed off, accepting, listening, or not. Many people seem to talk without noticing whether the other party is engaged or listening, but a person who is feeling and truly engaging reads the other person's body language and engages accordingly.

When a person approaches a horse just to pet it, they often disregard the horse's appearance, his telling signs, and his general needs. Many times, people go right up to the horse's face and crowd it, or immediately go for his lips and muzzle. This is the equivalent of hugging a person you've just met, which may not always be appropriate. It can also encourage a horse to crowd in return or lip or nip in response (which is why I discourage hand feeding treats).

My Morgan gelding Geronimo has a tendency to be pushy and nippy. He often approaches or follows people, crowding them a bit, and so, a well-meaning person may think he wants to be petted. In a short time, they'd find themselves next to a pushy monster with a bay muzzle and lips exploring their skin in a way they probably hadn't expected. Being petted this way doesn't make him happier or feel loved, it makes him frustrated and pushy. He is much happier when he receives space and is asked in turn to give space, too. When I do pet him, it's in a way that provides reassurance and helps to calm him.

My fiery chestnut mare, Dee, usually prefers not to be petted. She is not overly affectionate except in some occasions with some people. To be respectful of her, I pet her when it's appropriate and usually in a very slow and still way. Sometimes for her, a touch on the forehead or neck is just enough.

Horses' needs are so different, and each moment can require a different type of touch. As a kid, I grew up riding jumpers, and a 'pet' for them when they responded correctly was a type of smack on the neck. Sometimes, people pet their horses in brisk or hurried ways. A pet should be reassuring and peaceful for it to be beneficial, and it should have meaning.

Horses rely on feel to survive, which is why I prefer people not to pet my horses. Each touch should mean something. If I'm riding my horse, and I notice its attention is off somewhere but I need it back on me for a left turn, for example, I could initiate that left turn by a touch on the left side of its neck. Over-petting or rude petting dulls this essential form of communication out of the horse, making stronger aids necessary.

Most people know to ask before petting a strange dog. I rarely pet a dog, whether the owner okays it or not, until I see from the dog's body language he actually wants me to pet him, or it's the right thing for the situation. (For example, it may not be appropriate to pet a dog that wants to be petted in the presence of another dog who may be jealously guarding something, etc.) The same should go for people and horses; if it isn't yours, ask, and even if you are given permission, pay attention to the horse and pet in a way that doesn't encourage rudeness but does encourage peace and relaxation.

It's not that petting is bad. It's not that treats are bad. Talking isn't bad, and affection isn't bad. But if our words and touches are to be meaningful, then silence and quiet have to be a factor in our conversation, as well.

Questioning the 30-Day Start

Every clinician I've ridden with and every teacher I've taken lessons from touts the mantra: It takes the time it takes. Then why are our time constraints and demands still the horse's biggest enemies?

Years ago, it was generally accepted that training horses was a time-consuming event. Ray Hunt said, "As time goes on, all the little things will fall into line. We should be adjusting to fit the horse...You can't make it happen and you can't put a time limit on it...Sometimes the slower you go, the faster you learn."

Now, too often, there is a cheap, fast-food mentality to training horses. Trainers say essentially, 'You bring me a horse, and I'll produce a product,' rather than, 'I'll take time to develop an athlete.'

Horsemanship should be like fine cuisine, the kind that takes time to create before serving it.

As a rider and trainer, I'm often presented with the dilemma of a client wanting a horse started or fixed (sometimes both) in thirty days. It's a common timeframe for such a thing, but I wonder if it's really fair to the horse or the person to put a time limit on such an important and delicate event as the beginning or restart of a horse's riding life?

Years ago, I had a filly. I handled her gently from the day she was born. She never had any formal training until she was two. I just handled her routinely in a way that worked for both of us as needed. She was never scared, and everything seemed to flow smoothly.

At two, I saddled her for the first time. It was uneventful because she was used to all kinds of feelings on her body and around her.

At three, I rode her a time or two, which was also uneventful because she knew me, trusted me, and wasn't afraid.

At four, I began riding her seriously, and it was as if I had stepped onto an already-broke horse. Of course, she wasn't educated yet. But she was willing and relaxed. By her second ride, we were down the trail and moving cows. This filly's education was quite relaxed compared to the thirty-day colt starts I've been asked to do.

Paradoxically, taking your time often allows the process to speed up. Taking your time in this way increases their ability to relax, learn, and retain information.

After a year off, I returned my attention to the filly, and she was not too far behind where I'd left her. Often, horses that are pushed through a fast fix end up exploding for 'no apparent reason' or suddenly backsliding dramatically. Some of the horses I've seen go through training programs could one day be ridden but the next be barely touched.

Dr. Steve Peters and Maddy Butcher talked about this in a piece on the neurological low road and high roads of horse work: Danger is a normal part of life, but after trauma, the world is experienced with a different nervous system. Every encounter or event may be contaminated by the past.

In neuro-anatomy terms: The amygdala is the brain's smoke detector. It identifies whether or not incoming input is relevant to our survival. It does so quickly and automatically, with help of feedback from the hippocampus, a nearby structure that relates the new input to past experiences.

If the amygdala senses threat, it sends an immediate message to the hypothalamus and the autonomic nervous system to orchestrate a whole body response. It decides whether incoming information is a threat before we are consciously aware of the danger. By the time we realize what is happening, our body may already be on the move.

I can't help what happened in the past, but I can encourage new habits by the way I routinely, patiently encourage them not to hit the low road, i.e., by reacting with fear or aggression.

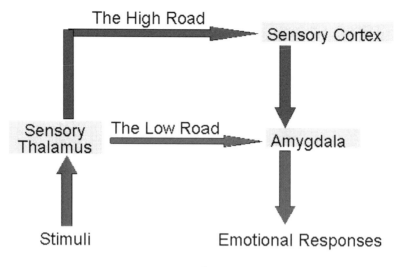

The High Road

Sensory Cortex

Sensory Thalamus

The Low Road

Amygdala

Stimuli

Emotional Responses

Courtesy of NY Times

Dr. Peters added, "When you think a horse is calm, it may actually be checked out. Its nervous system may be set at hyper-alert."

Two of my horses were originally training horses that came to me with pretty big issues. They were anxious. While they made progress, it seemed they still held quite a bit of tension. I took on both of the horses ultimately because of the amount of time it'd take to turn them around.

The minute I dropped any imposed time constraint and started playing around, an amazing thing happened. They relaxed enough to learn. They are both doing very well now, and I ask of them when I have time and as it works for them.

I'm not advocating that people send their horses to training indefinitely and spend all their money. But I think if horses and people both are going to be successful, changes need to happen:

- Riders need to pair themselves well with their horses.
- Riders need to ask if they are a good fit with their horses.
- Trainers need to be honest in their assessment of horse-rider pairs.

The six-year-old reactive mustang for the nervous rider is not a good fit. Taking such a horse like that under any timeframe is unfair to the horse and the rider if the rider's ability and lifestyle doesn't match the horse's needs.

The horse's personality and breeding should fit the rider's needs. If you want a quiet horse to enjoy on the trail, and you pick a good fit, it will take less time and money, and it will overall be a safer experience.

Another option is for riders to become more involved in the process. If they become involved in the horse's education before, during, and after their training program, they can have success. If they have a young or troubled horse, and they can't afford months of training, and they don't want to pair themselves with more suitable ones, then they'll have their work cut out for them.

Be fair to yourself and to your horse. Rise to the level of education your horse needs you to have. This might mean riding lessons, working with your horse and trainer (aside from training it), and spending some good time learning about your horse in general.

Good trainers don't create products on an assembly line. Each horse is unique in its needs, experiences, and expected jobs. Colt-starting competitions and wild horse makeovers give us the excitement of watching a young, green horse be gentled before our eyes. But to what end? Rushing the horse's education helps no one in the long term.

It's my opinion that we horse trainers carry the bulk of the burden in presenting a reasonable and fair expectation of what a horse can learn in a given amount of time. If we preach taking the time it takes, but then work our horse in a tight schedule, then we need either to admit we are hypocrites or to drop the schedule and offer something truly beneficial to the horse.

Finding a Good Coach

You're on the quest to find a good trainer. Or, maybe you already have a trainer, but are not sure if she is teaching good horsemanship and safety.

Regardless of your riding discipline, age, and ability, your confidence and success and those of your horse depend on a reliable and knowledgeable coach. Here are some aspects of a good trainer that I find important and that I look for when taking lessons.

A good trainer should:

- Teach horsemanship basics: day-to-day handling, problem solving, and confidence with horses.
- Teach a balanced seat and focuses on being in balance on a horse
- Focus on safety. Pairs appropriate level of horse to rider
- Provide safe school horses for riders to learn on
- Keep riders from advancing until their basics are solid. For example, teaching walk trot and canter before jumping, etc.
- Teach riders emergency techniques. For example, emergency dismount, how to stop a bolting horse, etc.
- Supervise keenly and always keep riders in awareness.
- Take an interest in the development of their horses and students; not just killing time to make a buck.
- Allow parents or friends to watch lessons, allows clients to watch training sessions.

- Teach in a way the student can understand or seek to find ways to demonstrate.
- Be interested in your horse's well-being and your safety
- Teach your horse to become safer and more dependable over time.
- Teach a rider to be more effective and clearer, and to understand their horse better.

A good trainer doesn't have to have all the answers or know everything. That just isn't possible. But an honest teacher will answer the best they can, say they don't know, or say they will see what they can find out.

Keep in mind that many trainers are very busy. Talk to your trainer to see if you need an appointment to watch or ask questions. Be considerate of their time and know that your horse or child is not her only priority. But do expect her to be completely focused when she is riding your horse or teaching your child.

Clients should:

- Watch training sessions or lessons.
- Listen intently in lessons and understand that safety relies on paying attention and carrying out instructions.
- Ask questions. Speak up when you don't understand or when you feel unsafe.
- Spend time reading and learning on your own time
- Take initiative.
- Make any health or physical problems crystal clear, so their instructor can keep you safe.

- Communicate wants, needs, and goals clearly.
- Take part in your horse's life and development. Come to farrier and vet appointments as possible.
- Stay in decent shape so you can follow trainer's directives and stay safe on a horse.

Additional notes: Some trainers are not teachers. Some teachers are not riders. And some trainers are not good communicators. None of this means they are bad at what they do. But if you are not getting what you need out of their work, you may need to have a conversation and be clear about what you need. Take your time and do your research to find the professional that fits your needs the best.

It is up to the clients to be sure their money is giving them what they need. If you feel you are not getting any of these things, it doesn't mean you have to bail immediately or that your teacher is not doing a good job. But consider sharing your thoughts or asking more questions.

Red flags & warning signs that it may be time to move on:

- Your trainer is dishonest with you or with other clients.
- Your instructor refuses to allow you to watch training sessions or lessons.
- After several clear conversations, your trainer is not meeting your needs.
- You are being repeatedly put in unsafe situations without adequate instruction or help.
- Your trainer gossips or bad mouths other clients or their horses.

- Your instructor talks on a cell phone during lessons or rides.

By keeping these key points in mind when choosing a professional, you'll help ensure your safety, your horse's well-being, and will help make riding what it should be: an educational and enjoyable endeavor.

Relaxation with the Aids

I stood in the pen with the anxious mustang, watching him pace back and forth, turning his head away to avoid the pressure of my presence. Every time I walked down toward his pen, before I even touched the gate, he would start pacing. I walked up quietly, getting as close as I was able to before he left. Where I stood, about 10 feet from him, he was not feeling so much pressure he had to leave but enough to make him uncomfortable. I waited, looking for him to let down and find relaxation with me there. Previously, when he'd stayed around with me that close, I'd turn around and leave him, letting him relax that way. But what I'd taught him was to find relaxation when I left. What I now wanted was for him to find relaxation with me here, then. In a few minutes, he left his head down and yawned. Instead of leaving, I stayed there a bit longer, letting him enjoy this mental softness he found with me.

In riding, as well, we should seek to help the horse find relaxation within a cue or movement. So much riding is based on escape and finding relief from avoidance. We ask our horse to go, and we kick with a leg or spur. When he reacts by moving forward, we release our leg, and he finds relief, not from our leg aid, but from the relief from taking our leg off. Similarly, we ask our horse to turn or stop, and he knows that to relieve pressure from the rein, he must move his body in a way to find relief away from that cue. For a nervous or worried horse, a cue—be it leg, rein, or anything—can get him tense and reacting and then rewarded by the release of a cue for reacting in tension. Just like the mustang finding relief when I leave, reaction-based release teaches the horse that he gets rewarded for tension, and he finds this tension more and more often while riding.

Sometimes in dressage, we hear words like 'get the horse in front of the leg' or 'get him off your aids.' A horse that is in 'front' of your aids is one that is escaping a driving cue, leaving the rider behind, with late timing and inability to influence the horse where he is at that moment. A horse that is 'off' the aids is one that reacts to the leg or hand. A horse that you teach to come to the aids and find suppleness and relaxation learns to find peace with you. This horse is not only a joy to ride but also truly safe, because he wants to be with you, under your seat and with your hand, and feels soft and relaxed mentally and physically. One that reacts to escape a cue is moving in tension, and a tense horse can never be completely safe.

What I hope to ride and train into a horse is a supple and relaxed horse. I'd really like my cue to be the thing that brings relaxation to that horse, like the mustang stretching his neck and yawning while I stood by him. This means the rider asks without tension in her body and, while asking the horse with a relaxed and well timed feel, leaves that feel there for him to follow, stay with, and enjoy. There, of course, are small releases, and every conversation is dynamic, but the leg, seat, and hand are there for the horse to feel and be comfortable. The horse learns to feel your seat, your leg, your hand, not to escape it but to seek and stay with it for comfort, because it promotes relaxation. Then you have a horse that sees you and finds comfort, feels you and reaches for you because you have always provided peace within the movements, not after they are finished.

Micro-Managing vs. Guiding

My primary love is dressage. I love everything about it—developing the horse as an athlete, using a thoughtful process to create a more balanced horse, and achieving the persnickety, delicate balance of all my body parts working in alignment with the horse's. It could just be my temperament. I enjoy the quiet process of slow daily work to create a bigger, better picture. Nothing too fast, and everything is subtle. Like art, every detail counts to create a masterpiece.

One of the primary downfalls of dressage in my observation is the tendency of many riders to over-school and micromanage.

I've ridden many schooling horses who had to be 'held together' or they would fall out of balance. If my leg was not constantly driving, if my outside rein was not constantly holding, the horse would either not collect, would fall in, or would speed up, slow down, fall on the forehand, etc. A horse like that to me is not a pleasure to ride, and I can guarantee the horse is not having a pleasurable time being ridden, either.

On the other hand, a horse that is ridden too loose (not just referring to rein length here) without guidance from the rider's focus, seat, and reins can become wobbly and frustrated. This is a horse that runs the risk of being over-corrected because he is not clear on what is expected of him. For example, a rider not guiding as she rides past the gate may find that her horse gravitates toward it.

In my yoga class, we are taught how to put our bodies into each pose. Some of them are difficult for me, requiring strength and flexibility in areas I don't have yet. My instructor explains how to get into the pose and keeps an eye on each of us to make sure our bodies stay in correct alignment, with a little wiggle room for those of us who lack flexibility. She places emphasis on correct alignment in all poses above anything else. For example, in a forward fold, it's essential to keep a flat back, so if you can't yet touch your nose to your knees with straight legs, you would bend your knees to maintain a flat back. She guides each of us, helping us work toward bettering ourselves, but she doesn't nag or hold us up. What good would it do us if she coddled, forced, or held us in position? We each are working toward better understanding our own bodies and developing a feel for when we're in correct alignment. It doesn't help us become more balanced if we just do what she says without any real understanding of why or how to get there.

I think there is a perfect balance between guiding the horse and setting it up for success and micro-managing. They should have enough contact and feel from the person to have a clear idea of where to go, what speed to take, and what shape to assume. It should be like a continuous conversation between horse and rider, with the rider leading a second ahead of the horse. That means the rider has to have awareness about where her horse's thoughts are headed, what is happening around them, and be able to predict and respond to him before he has taken them completely out of where the rider had intended. A fair rider will not wait until the horse is across the arena headed to the gate or headed to its friend before she corrects. That would be like having a teenager and telling them, do whatever you want, or worse not paying attention to them at all, and waiting till they were in trouble to punish them.

A good horse person heads off trouble and prevents it from happening when possible. Better than that, they continually set the horse up for success, trying to offer a path for him to take so his thoughts can be on what to do, rather than on what not to do. If riders can continually convey speed, direction, and body shape to their horses in a way that's fair, they can prevent lots of problems from creeping up. When riders become good leaders and partners, they find fewer problems with horses drifting toward the gate, trying to head back to the barn, or being buddy sour. This is because they are providing the horse with all the information he needs to do what is expected.

Cross Ties

I recently sold a horse and delivered him to his new barn. I relayed the basic information of the four-year-old gelding to his new owner: walk, trot, canter, trailers, clips, so-so, etc. Basic four year old stuff. I watched the horse get settled in, said my goodbyes, and headed back to the truck, when she said, "Oh, by the way, I forgot to ask, and this is probably a dumb question. He cross ties, right?"

"Uh, not really. Never done it," I said.

"Um, so how do I tie him?"

She stared at me blankly for a second, and I explained I rarely tie my horses for tacking up and routine handling. I prefer to teach my horses to stand on their own accord as much as possible, though I do tie on some occasions and believe horses should know how to tie safely. But cross-tying as an option is something that doesn't even occur to me.

What bothers me about cross-tying is that to the horse, it doesn't make sense. When simply tied, if the horse is educated to release himself off of pressure, he can learn to stand safely without pulling back and getting himself into trouble. He has enough space usually to figure out how to untrack his hindquarters and step forward. With a cross tie setup, the horse has pressure on both sides of his face, nowhere to go forward without pressure, and nowhere to go backward without pressure. Depending on the cross ties and their length, sometimes just standing there in the center maintains a steady pressure on the horse's face. (Those clips are usually pretty heavy.) Horses understand and learn by seeking relief, either from pressure, pain, or some type of stress, and the cross ties don't provide a horse with a clear path toward this relief. There isn't a place where he can stand calmly with slack in the rope generally, and the potential for injury and panic is high.

If startled, upset, frustrated, antsy, and so on, the horse naturally wants to move. Imagine something behind him startling or spooking him. His instinct is to go forward, but in cross ties he meets pressure from both sides of his face. The only option for him to relieve this pressure is to go up, and depending on the footing (which in many barns here is concrete), his potential for slipping or flipping backward is quite high. I've seen too many horses flip over in cross ties ever to consider this a safe option in my book again. If something startles him from in front of him, moving backward into the cross ties can be just as dangerous. Even a horse that has become used to the cross ties and can stand there quietly learns to lean into this pressure, making him heavier on the lead rope, heavy on the bridle, and heavy in his mind. He's been dulled through repetitive lack of relief from pressure.

If your interest in cross ties was to keep your horse still and to prevent him from moving away from something he isn't interested in, like a saddle, a vaccine, a trim, and so on, there are more meaningful ways to educate a horse to stand relaxed. Cross ties in these situations make him feel trapped, and if he really isn't interested in standing still, he will find a way to move anyway. Not to mention, if your goal is a relationship based on trust and communication, trapping your horse and forcing him to stand still is not a great way to achieve that.

If I had to round up my students and force them to stay and listen in a lesson, it would probably reflect a bit about me and the way in which I present information to them, than my students. I hope they come because they're interested and stay because it helps them, not because they feel they must. If a horse can be taught in a way he can understand, he'll often stand there on his own accord. Horses are generous that way.

In horsemanship, we seek lightness, and if your interest is working off a feel, cross ties can only muddy this goal. In dressage, jumping, and many western disciplines, we seek 'forward, straight, and balanced.' The cross ties can take only the forward out by teaching the horse to lean into pressure and discourage his forward movement. Not all disciplines seek this, but I have no interest in disciplines that disregard the horse's natural movement, so they don't need to be mentioned.

Everything is closely tied together when working with horses, from the way he catches to the way he handles on the ground to how he rides. If a balanced, quiet ride is what you seek, then it starts here, on the ground, in all the tiny little details. If you can take the time to teach your horse to stand relaxed, you'll be amazed at the difference in your horse's demeanor in general.

Young Horses

Starting horses is all about giving them a good foundation for the rest of their lives. When I get a horse to start, I want to make sure it's exposed to as much as I can to help prepare it for its future as a riding horse and instill confidence and curiosity at a young age. I know I can't prepare it for everything it will come across, but if I can get a good mix of curiosity and confidence in other things, I know that colt will have what it needs to tackle new obstacles it hasn't yet seen. Regardless of its future, whether it's a dressage horse, jumper, cutting horse, trail horse, you name it, I believe every young horse should know how to walk, trot, and canter on a loose rein, ride out alone and with friends on the trail, and move a cow.

When a young horse is getting started, he can be almost overwhelmingly flooded with new information quickly. He has to learn to carry a saddle, wear a bridle and bit, and a rider, all within a short time. Then he has to handle learning to interpret the scary and funny feeling in his mouth when the rider tries to direct him, all while managing weight on his back. Then he gets exposed to new and scary things all the time—new places, obstacles, scary corners in the arena, cows, whatever. It's all new, and the horse is being flooded, hopefully in a productive and confidence boosting way with information that he has to digest and learn to handle. Starting, no matter how well you go about it, can be stressful on a horse.

Young horses are learning to balance themselves, and you'll often see them move about in silly or awkward ways. Their bodies aren't fully developed, and they can experience fear or concern while carrying a rider as they try to find their balance with not just their own feet but with extra weight on top that may or may not be centered all the time.

I believe strongly that horses that are raised outside in a healthy herd dynamic and are exposed to varied terrain and situations are much easier to start. Young horses that have to balance in different types of footing or surfaces and have to manage uneven and hilly terrain have a better sense of balance and of their surroundings. This is totally natural for a horse. Unfortunately, many young horses are born in stalls, brought into stalls daily, and spend most of their time in small, groomed pens, and are handled in sterile arenas with flat and soft footing. This offers the young horse no advantage in his development, and as he gets started and has to learn to balance a rider and himself, he is often more nervous and less capable than a young horse raised outside in a more natural environment.

Horses that are raised in 'unpredictable' environments also learn more quickly, as they have to adapt faster and learn to trust their instincts. The stall-raised young horse is often fly sprayed, blanketed, and shielded from unpleasant stimulus; therefore, he never has to adapt to survive. Humans remove his ability and then get on his back, expecting him to perform at peak levels and learn quickly.

If you want to have a super learner, an athlete, and a brave and curious horse, do him the favor of being outside without interference. Let him deal with bugs, wind, hills, and rain. Let him manage around the holes in the pasture. Horses and holes have evolved together since their existence, and horses have not been wiped out yet because of them. It will not only make him healthier, happier, and more mentally balanced, but it will make him a better learner and better athlete, too.

To Catch a Horse

Why doesn't my horse want to get caught?

Next to trailer loading, catching a horse is one of the most frequent scenarios in which we lose our emotional control. Every horse owner knows the frustration: You go out to catch your beloved horse, and he wants nothing to do with you. He turns tail and runs.

There are many popular methods for catching a hard-to-catch horse, from bribing with treats to chasing him until he 'chooses' to get caught. But when catching horses, it's important to invest in the process and consider what you're teaching in those moments.

Chasing a horse that is hard to catch is counter-productive. If he's running out of fear, chasing him adds more fear. If he's running out of habit, chasing him encourages that habit. Some people say they are giving the horse the choice between being run and being caught.

Imagine using that tactic on a friend. They don't want to be near you, so you say, either you let me be near you or I am going to make your life unpleasant. It doesn't sound too good, does it? They might choose to get caught when their lungs are burning, but they haven't stopped because they want to be caught. They just don't want to be uncomfortable anymore. It would break my heart if my friends didn't want to be around me. But punishing them would only make the situation worse. I would need to look at why they don't want to be around me.

So, why doesn't your horse want to get caught?

- Your approach to catching them doesn't work for him. You may be walking in too fast, too hard, or haltering him in a way that irritates or just doesn't fit.
- He may associate you or other people with fear, drudgery, and pain.
- He doesn't associate getting caught with positive feelings, growth, and relaxation.
- It may be habit for him to leave you during catching.
- He may be afraid.

Refusing to get caught has nothing to do with disrespect or poor behavior. Teaching a horse to be caught softly has everything to do with human approach.

So, how do you catch that horse who offers you his tail?

When catching a horse, I ask myself what I want the horse to be learning. I want him to learn to draw in to me, to find relief and relaxation with me, and, most importantly, to build a relationship.

When I go to catch a horse that might be worried or uninterested, the first thing I want to do is teach him to engage and become interested. I'll reward him by taking the pressure off (leaving him entirely or just a little, depending on the horse and the moment) any time he tunes in, in other words look toward me, or step toward me.

Kevin is an example of a once hard-to-catch horse. Kevin was older, without much handling, and he was suspicious and scared to death of nearly everything. Catching him could be tricky.

When I went into the pen to catch him, I made sure I didn't move too quickly. But I also made sure I wasn't too still. I moved as fluidly as I could.

When I entered his pen, he would snort and trot off. Rather than chase him off, I would quietly follow him, keeping my energy in a 'following' feel, so as not to push him more. I kept my footsteps soft. I tried to see where Kevin was going to go next and sometimes get there first. When he looked toward me or became curious, I would back up. Repetitions of this action cemented the 'draw.' My goal wasn't to catch Kevin until he was ready to be caught. My goal was to teach him to become interested.

Sometimes, Kevin would step toward me. If this happened, I would back up. Eventually, he started to follow me, and if I stopped, he came up behind me and would investigate and sniff me. This built his confidence.

Chasing or approaching head-on would have been entirely too much pressure for him, and counter-productive. Once I could approach him, I prepared him for being touched by 'air petting' his face without actually touching him. In this way, he wouldn't be alarmed by my reaching out toward his face. As I moved closer, my hand made contact with his face without any change in the motion of my arm, and he didn't worry. Then, I prepared him for the look and feel of being haltered by doing the same on the side of his face, under his jaw and above his ears. I wanted to keep things smooth so that no part of the process scared him or gave him reason to lose trust.

After some time, catching Kevin became easy. But I maintained that ease by making sure every session with him ended in relaxation of mind and body, and that when I turned him loose, I didn't scare him off. As I unhaltered him, I made sure to draw him in and walk away before he did. I try to constantly reward the draw, and once that became habit, Kevin was solid to catch.

But it isn't enough to just teach horses how to be caught. We need to make sure every time we work with them, we leave them feeling positive, relaxed, and better than when we found them in the pasture.

I want them to think when they see me, 'there's the person who makes me feel better than eating grass with my friends.' If you know anything about horses, that's a tall order, but it's a challenge I found worthy of my time.

Is Your Horse a Freeloader?

Ray Hunt said, "The first time you ride a horse, he'll cost you money. The second time he'll hold his own. The third ride, he's on the payroll." I've thought about this quote a lot over the years. It has a different meaning to me now than it did years ago. The young horses I started always came up with some resistance to my leg or rein or body aids during the first week of riding, and I always figured they needed more time to sort things out.

This month, I've had somewhat of an epiphany as I've gone through starting the group of young horses at the Bar T. Before riding them, all the work I did with them on the ground was directly related to riding. I asked them to carry themselves in the posture I want to ride them in, and looked for lightness and relaxation with my cues. But beyond this, I also asked them really to be a part in what I was asking. I asked myself, how can I get this horse not just to accept what I'm doing, but to be a part of it?

When I caught a horse, I asked him to participate by facing up, lowering his head, softening his poll, and tipping his head toward me. Not forcing him to do these things but to find them through relaxation and learn to get in these habits. When saddling, I stopped going around the horse to get to the cinches but moved him around me, moving the shoulders around the front end and putting himself in place for me to cinch it up.

I asked my horse to lead up to a block, fence, or wherever I was standing for mounting. I most definitely asked him to stay still when I mounted and dismounted. I asked him to find relaxation in whatever I was asking and to participate rather than tolerate. This resulted in better first rides with less trouble and fear on his end (and mine), a better relationship between what I'd taught on the ground and what I was asking for under saddle, and a working horse in fewer rides.

I have a group of colts right now that on their second and third rides were walking through water, going out on the trail, opening fences, and loading cows up onto a trailer. The reason these colts were so handy and relaxed so soon was because they'd already been contributing since Day 1. Everything we did under saddle was just the next thing from what they'd already been doing. It wasn't a shock or big change from pre-riding life to going under saddle.

I think of a lot of the bosses I've had. In jobs where bosses told me what to do, I complied because I knew my paycheck depended on it. But I had to be asked, and I did only what I was asked, nothing more. In jobs where my bosses asked me to participate and treated me like a partner in work, I felt valued and therefore offered much more. I noticed things that needed to be done and did them without being asked, because I was part of the whole, not just being directed and waiting to get done and go home. I believe horses feel the same, and at the risk of anthropomorphizing them, I feel that horses that are asked to take part and have jobs feel a sense of pride in their work. I see this when my colts get confident after moving a cow, ponying another horse, or opening a gate. They know they contributed to something and feel confident about their ability.

I feel sad for horses that just get ridden around in arenas, show pens, and trails where they are just asked to do, perform, go, stop, turn. They are treated like robots, like slaves, not like thinking, intelligent beings with so much to offer. I hear people blame their horses regularly, but what I hear when they do that are excuses for their poor horsemanship: "He's too much of a baby to do that." "My horse hates water. He'd never go through that." "That's all well and good on a gelding, but try doing that with a mare." "Oh, but he's an Arab/Warmblood/show horse/donkey/mule/whatever." What people are saying when they insult their horse is that they are afraid and/or ignorant and unwilling to change.

So, is your horse a freeloader? As my teacher Alicia Byberg said to me once, "Pet your horse and slap yourself." I still haven't heard better advice to this day.

Why a Horse Says "No"

In the philosophy of horsemanship following Ray Hunt and Tom and Bill Dorrance, there is a common saying that when working with horses, we make the right thing easy and the wrong thing hard. The hope is that the horses will pick up the same idea we had, and we can go along together. But if we aren't forcing horses to do anything and allowing them to make decisions, occasionally 'no' will come up as an answer. It's at this point I believe real horsemen and women are made. There are many out there putting on cowboy hats talking philosophy, talking about not making the horse a slave, talking about physical and mental lightness. But when presented with 'no' as an answer from the horses, the real horse men and women get pondering, not forcing.

At this point, we need to analyze the piece that isn't working. Once we've identified the 'why,' we can go back down the line a bit and work to create a horse that feels confident in trying to seek what we seek, or decide if what we seek is appropriate for him at all. Here are a few reasons a horse could say no:

—It could be the horse lacks confidence. If, for example, we ask him to go on a trail ride and leave the farm when his sense of security comes from his friends and the barn, leaving without the tools to cope would be too much. He would need some foundation to draw from. Try asking for smaller, easier tasks that he can succeed at and build toward the big task.

—It could be the horse doesn't understand our request. If our position or cues are muddy, choppy, unclear, or poorly timed, he would have no idea what to do with the conflicting information.

—If what we ask brings the horse's need to defend himself up, his answer could be no. A horse values safety first and foremost, and if our request interferes with his need to stay safe, 'no' would be the obvious answer. Or, if our way of asking brings about his self-preservation, or if he has a pattern of feeling the need to defend himself from previous experiences.

- Horse lacks overall respect, and/or human makes guidelines sloppy or unclear. We can see this a lot in trailer loading or leading up to a mounting block.
- The person asks the horse to lead up straight, but he swings his hind end around away from the desired area. If the person waits till the horse is already crooked, they have waited too long, and the horse has received a release for going to this place, which they will build on. At this point, the horse believes that is where he should be and continues to do it, but better. So, their 'no' is not really a no to what you want, but a yes to what they inadvertently requested.

If we are going to create thoughtful horses with honest answers, we need to look at our foundation when these situations come up, and they will. Have we given the horse enough experience to do what we ask? Have we given him confidence? Have we refined our timing to and skill enough to be sure what we ask is clear to him? Have we taught him to fight or to try, to think, and are we patient enough to wait for him to find it himself, instead of making him? If we seek lightness, it can't be forced. It must be mental before it can be physical, which means never forcing a 'yes.'

Are Trainers Invested in the Process?

Lately, I've asked myself, 'What do I really know? And does it really work for the horse?'

After long doses of reflection and experimentation, I've changed my training practices. Here's what I'm finding: There are plenty of ways to 'get things done,' and there can be plenty of pressure to rush a horse. Having trained for the public for a decade now, I've worked with thousands of horses. That's thousands of opportunities for me to learn from a horse and for him to tell me what does and doesn't work. I'm a big proponent of listening to a horse first, a silver-lining consequence of listening to people before horses for too long.

I've seen too many horses get the losing end of a deal when it comes to training. Trainers trying to prove they can turn a horse around faster than others or take a bronc-ier horse than others. I've seen horses flipped over, injured, scared, run off, and lose confidence more every day. Rushed training—in which horses flip over, get hurt, scared, or lose their confidence—is more about boosting the trainer's ego than helping the horse. Yet, "I can't put a time limit on helping this horse" is an unpopular answer, and trainers fear they will lose business. As one trainer told me, "Time is money. The client wants results. If we don't get it done, they're gonna take it somewhere else to someone who will do worse." To me, this reaction is unacceptable. As trainers purporting to be 'in it for the horse,' we simply must do better.

At Brent Graef's Young Horse Handling Class, I visited with Brent and his wife, Kris, about training time. Brent halter-starts yearlings from the Singleton Ranch and later helps start the same colts as two year olds. The Singleton Ranch is one of the largest ranches in the country, producing many high-money earners in the National Cutting Horse Association.

Here's part of our conversation:

Brent: How does this work compared to what you're used to? (Referring to the smoothness of the unperturbed yearlings)

Amy: Well, it's a lot quieter. I'm used to a lot more feathers flying. As a colt starter, I've been told I need to ride a buck better or get a real cowboy to do it.

Brent: Some colt starters are bronc riders, and they're using the colts for bronc-riding practice. That's not the kind of person I'd like to ride my colt. I'd like him to not buck. He doesn't need to do that. That's the first thing I tell the guys at the Singleton's. They'll have new people that are coming in that are cowboys. I'll say we're gonna try to keep the horse out of trouble. We're not here to make the horse buck. If you start making him buck, you're out. Real simple deal.

Amy: If somebody asks you how long halter-starting takes or how long starting a colt takes or how long it takes to fix XYZ problem, how do you answer that question?

Brent: When I was starting them for the public, we got thirty days. Some of them would stay for sixty, but we could usually only get paid for thirty. You could expect fifteen to twenty rides. That's what you'll probably get. It's not like you'll have a grandkid horse in that time.

Brent: Each person has different skills. Things could take longer or shorter depending on those, and your set up, and how much time you have in a day. There's really not a 'how long it takes.'

Amy: So, do you charge the same fee for troubled horses as you do other ones?

Brent: I don't take troubled horses. I used to. But I'd tell people they were looking at at least a four- to six-month deal. But now we just take halter-starting horses.

Amy: So, how do you get around time constraint expectations with your clients?

Brent: No matter how long it takes, we charge a flat fee. And we have a money back guarantee. If they don't like our work, they don't pay.

Amy: And how do you manage the fact that your training horses are going to be one way with you and another with your clients?

Brent: Well, that's what led to the clinics. When I'd take in a problem horse, I'd fix it up and send it home. The people would bring it back in a couple months with the same problem, and I'd think, that was fixed! So, I'd fix it up again. It took me a little while to realize it's not the horse causing the problem. So, with the colts, they'd have to come ride with me, and with a problem horse, they'd have to come ride with me more than with a colt. I'd show them things that were causing the problems and tell them they had to quit doing that.

Kris Graef: Some people say quick colt starting isn't good for the horse, but it depends. It may be bad, it may not be. It depends on how you do it. You don't want the horse to get bored, you don't want certain personalities to take over. It goes faster with a good set up, and being able to ride your colts in a group is a huge advantage.

Amy: Doing it quickly with good preparation is not the same as doing it quickly, and I think that's something the public doesn't always get to see. Thanks for the great answers.

Brent: You bet.

SECTION THREE:
Stories

My Saddle

My Saddle
My Office
My Throne
My platform for learning, daydreaming, and making life decisions
It has seen countless horses—rangy, fancy, green, dull, troubled, and dead broke.
$500 horses and $100,000 horses—They're all the same, breathing fire, tearing up the earth beneath my saddle.
It's seen snow, wind, rain, and sunshine.
Tears, sweat and both horse and my own blood.
I've cried in it.
Laughed in it.
Fallen in and out of love in it.
I've been lifted up into the heavens with magical rides and unseated from it.
The slab of leather between me and my horse gives me the ability to grow, change, and become the rider and person I always wanted to be.

Evening in a Field

I walk through the field with the setting sun on my back
Cattle dog at my heels,
Cows on the horizon starting back
Wondering about me with the same curiosity
My eye finds in them.
The day's warmth spreads the smell of grass and manure,
Stirring feelings of comfort, familiarity, and peace.
I listen to the jingle of my pup's collar as she roots around
For evidence of interesting animals passing through this field.
The budding trees sway in an early spring breeze.
The birds seem to realize the gift of this good weather and
Celebrate by joining in the frogs' spring songs.
In the evening light I check on the animals,
Standing in awe of the peace of their existence,
And steal some for myself, too.
I smell my own sweat from a day of work,
Streaks made in the dirt on my skin.
My hands are dark from the sun and
I am profoundly happy.

Going Against the Stream:
Connecting the Lead Rope to the Feet

A few of my clients keep their horses out at their places, and I drive around periodically to ride them. Usually, I'm able to make it out there when everyone is at work during the daytime; consequently, I'm locked out of the house. Now when you drink coffee all morning and ride horse after horse, you give up a bit of your dignity and go where you can, lest it be by accident in the saddle. The price of a quick ride doesn't include a thorough saddle cleaning, so like many of my horse-riding gal pals, I have no problem using a stall, horse trailer, or wooded area to 'powder my nose.'

This particular day, I'd just finished riding one horse and had caught the next one when the urge struck me. These horses lived in a huge field, and I'd walked clear down to the other end to catch him, so I wasn't about to let him go, take care of business, and come back to see if he was still interested in a ride. The only place within non-pants-wetting distance was the run-in shed, so the gelding and I trucked our way over there. The shed was out in the open, facing a neighboring house's front room window.

I decided to use the gelding for cover and squatted in the corner with him positioned right in front of me. The perplexed gelding stared me down, probably judging me and thinking about all the bad things he would say about me to his friend when he got done with me. I had just dropped trou' and was midstream when the other horse went tearing past the shed down the hill. My training horse started to jig and dance, wanting to be with his friend. The lead rope was quickly coming tight in my hand.

I had to act quickly, trying to do groundwork and pull my pants up at the same time, praying the neighbors didn't see. I have to say I was pretty impressed with my little dance, left hand on my belt and right hand on the lead rope, tipping my horse's nose in to untrack his hindquarters without even peeing on myself. On second thought, maybe the neighbors SHOULD be watching this, I thought. I may be a sorry hand at roping, but at least I was able to stop midstream to pull my pants and get a hold of a fire-breathing dragon, all without the slack coming out of the rope. Loads of practice at this when my pants were securely fastened helped make this possible.

And that, my friends, is why connecting the feet to the lead rope is important, because we just never know when we're gonna need that lead rope to mean something.

Geronimo

Anyone who knows me knows I don't shy away from a challenge. I'm also a work addict, and I love a project. I really enjoy working with difficult horses, but I hate to admit sometimes when they're mine, it's harder to keep it objective. Geronimo has been difficult, and anyone who knows him knows he is strong-willed, intelligent to a creepy level, and impossible to coerce into anything. If he's going to do it, there's going to be a reason that he understands, and he's going to have to get behind that reason first. I appreciate that about him, and I understand it, because I'm very similar. We have a mutual distaste for fluff or anything that wastes our time, and we don't like to socialize with people who have agendas. That's one of the reasons why I love my Goliath-in-a-tiny-package. But when it comes to our relationship, he eyes me with the same scrutiny as he does others, which I have a hard time not taking personally.

I've tried to relay to him that cantering is a valuable exercise, and after a summer of exploding, refusing, bucking, cross cantering, and shutting down completely when asked, he finally did canter both leads. But he didn't put his heart in it, and my gorgeous, athletic and nice-moving little devil gave me the worst, most uncomfortable canter every time I asked. All 14.2

hands of him would stiffen, his neck would tighten, and his hind end would sort of drop and scoot, rather than engage to lift his shoulders. It felt like riding in a truck with no shocks going 60mph down a rocky gravel road. And then I'd turn him loose and watch him canter off to his friends, neck beautifully arched, hind end lowered, at a lovely, rhythmic gait.

If I were a cartoon, I think steam would have come out my ears. I'd agonize over what I was doing wrong. I'd try harder the next time and make it worse, then I'd ease up on him, thinking I had gone overboard, and that would make it worse than ever. I had a hard time finding the balance between pushing him to try, because he rarely did, and being too easy on him at a level where he was comfortable.

So, the other day, we're going through our normal routine— bracey groundwork followed by a warmup of alternating between lurching behind the bit, grabbing the bit and straining his neck, and an occasional, delightfully soft moment. Some transitions and then right to the canter, like Jec Ballou suggested, "Don't avoid it because it's ugly," she said. "He's got to learn to go through it to get to the other side." Ugh. I would much rather avoid it forever, and maybe wake up one day and find him magically perfect, but here goes nothing. So, I ask him to canter left lead, his harder one. He goes for his choppy trot, and I ask him to soften and slow and try again. Left lead, giraffe neck, stiff, choppy, irregular rhythm. I'm trying to fix it, and BAM! He goes a** over teakettle, launching me forward where I promptly fill my mouth, front of my shirt and pants with sand. I roll over and look up. I can see him roll toward me, thankfully missing me, and stand up.

Geronimo is of the pensive sort, and he stood there looking down at me as I looked up at him. Normal horses would have been scared, maybe, or worried about what had just happened, but he just looked down at me, not even breathing hard. I brushed the sand off the exterior of my clothes, spat out the bulk of what was in my mouth, and gritted the rest while I put my foot back in the stirrup and got back on.

I asked for left lead canter again, and this time, Geronimo placed each foot carefully and thoughtfully and lowered his croup for an uphill transition. He sneezed and blew in his canter, whereas before, he had held his breath, huffing and puffing like he was an obese person waddling after a donut. I could have cried, and I think I might have. At this point, I couldn't tell because I was covered in dirt and horse hair and sweat with my hair matted under my helmet. I was sitting on my incredible horse who was cantering, and it was comfortable, and I was so happy.

What's really interesting about this whole deal is that I had considered laying him down and just hadn't for a myriad reasons, but I guess it was time for him to be laid down, and he was, and it worked. Since then, Geronimo still isn't perfect, but he's trying, and I feel like I went up a bit in the food chain in his mind. I guess we both needed a little change of perspective.

To My Mare, with Thanks and Apologies

The sun gleams through the mare's flaxen mane, setting it on fire with light. She stretches her head down and yawns, licking her lips and blinking. I bury my face in her neck, smelling the most familiar scent—perfumy, musky, feminine, and pure; my first horse, my very own. She smells like sunshine and air and hay. As I stroke her neck, I run my fingers over layers of my own mistakes, a map of my learning; muscles misshapen through incorrect use of her body and ignorance. I wish I could have known then what I know now, and I hope I keep doing better to make up for my wrongdoing through not knowing.

Some new muscles peek through, and her neck and tail hang relaxed now. With her relaxed eyes and lips, she tells me I've hooked onto something better that works for her.

I've learned more from this mare than any other horse. At times, I can't understand why she even gave a quarter of what she did, but the heart of a horse is grateful and giving. With half a chance at being understood, they'll give what they can muster and more. So many times she's filled in for me, where she's been where I needed her to be when my timing was late.

I promised to do right by my mare the day I got her. I've fumbled, struggled, and tried too hard for years, arrogantly believing I was fixing her, before I was able to see she was teaching me to have better timing, a better understanding, patience, balance, and feeling for a horse's needs. To relax and let it take the time it takes, and to be a better human being to have something to offer her in return and the next horses that come along needing help and helping me.

Bellus

Bellus, a ten-year-old Lusitano gelding, came to me in January with a rearing problem. He was schooling third level dressage (which involves advanced lateral movements, flying changes, and extended gaits, requiring balance, rhythm and self-carriage) at the time, and his trainers were fed up with him.

"Everything else was fine," they said, except when Bellus decided he was done, he would stop and rear. Bellus was brought to us so we could "fix up that one little problem," then he could go back to schooling. He was expected to start getting good scores in shows, and then they could sell him.

Yet everything else was not fine. In the short time that Bellus was in training, the poor horse was exposed to quite a different world than he was used to.

Bellus was used to going in a stall. As a stallion late to being gelded and having been isolated in his earlier years, his social skills were underdeveloped, and he was kept separately from other horses.

He came off the trailer, wearing shipping boots and a fleece-lined halter. He snorted at the cows over the fence, and the cows snorted back at him. At the ranch, he did not live in a stall, but in a private paddock next to five other horses.

His clipped coat stood on end when the wind picked up or when it rained. Because of his prior grooming, I needed to blanket him when the weather was bad.

At first, Bellus struggled to adjust. I rode him out on the trails, through water, with the cows, and I did very little dressage. I wanted to avoid dressage because the gelding had been drilled half to death with the movements which a) were not done correctly and b) had no meaning or value in his life. The way dressage had been presented to him had not given him better balance and relaxation; it had only made him backward and resentful. I thought it would be better for him mentally to avoid much schooling in the arena and learn a different type of balance. The gelding had so little confidence on the trail that he shook with trepidation and could not will himself to go forward.

With the cows, he trembled and tried to whirl around or stop and rear when he saw them. His response to everything he didn't understand or thought he couldn't do was to shut down. In doing this, he'd sull up, slam on the front end hard, and refuse to move, then come up in the front end.

He had no idea how to use his body properly as he had always been pushed into a false 'collected' frame. He had always been ridden on a tight rein, spurred, and whipped into the contact as he continually lost his forward momentum. Shutting down became the only option he could summon.

When I was riding him on a loose rein, he tripped, stumbled, rushed, and jolted to a stop. He did not know how to handle not being held up by someone's reins and driven into them. He had no balance of his own, and without being confined by the reins, he fell forward on his front end heavily. He felt unbalanced and often panicked. He did not have any of the fundamental qualities that a well-started horse should have had: confidence, try, balance, ability to go forward, and relaxation. In my mind, without these qualities, Bellus had no business competing at third-level dressage.

After a month in training, Bellus made marked improvements. He would walk, trot, and canter in a forward manner on a loose rein. He would ride out on the trails, and I had many beautiful long trots with him where he loosened and lowered his scrunched-up neck and lifted his back, extending his stride over the hilly fields.

In the minds of his owners/trainers, however, Bellus was still being a long way from where they wanted him. Many trainers had strung his owners along, trying to do the right thing, and after years of spending on trainers who had only muddled him up worse, they were at the end of their rope. They asked me to take him, and I was glad to do so.

My first order of business was to improve his physical and mental well-being. I pulled his shoes off and turned him out onto a field with my three-year old filly. He was pretty tender-footed after having worn shoes for his entire riding life. As for his living situation, I think Bellus must have thought he had died and gone to heaven.

His life for the past few months has been his first real experience being a horse: eating grass, galloping, dozing in the sun, swatting at flies, grooming his filly friend, and relaxing.

CLOSING THOUGHTS

If there's anything I've learned from working with horses, it's that I haven't learned enough. I'm constantly amazed at what each new horse has to teach me. I used to believe there would be a time where I would finally have "it," this magical time where I wouldn't struggle anymore because I just understood what needed to be done at all times.

I've since come to learn that learning is endless. Each new horse shows me something new. The challenge is to stay present and humble enough to hear the message. What it comes down to, I believe, is what Ray Hunt said: "you're not working on your horse, you're working on yourself." So, my friends, I urge you to stay open enough to listen, bold enough to try, and to learn to love the journey.

RESOURCES

Dorrance, Bill & Desmond, Leslie. (1999). *True Horsemanship Through Feel.*
Guilford, CT: The Lyons Press.

Hunt, Ray (1987). *Think Harmony With Horses: An In-Depth Study of*
Horse/Man Relationship. Bruneau, ID: Give-It-A-Go Books.

Peters, Stephen & Black, Martin. (2012). *Evidence Based Horsemanship.*
Shelbyville, KY: Wasteland Press.

Ballou, Jec Aristotle. (2019) http://ww.jecballou.com

Graef, Brent. (2019) http://www.brentgraef.com

Landman, Alicia. (2019) http://bybergequestrian.com

Printed in Great Britain
by Amazon